Vengeance
in a
Small Town

Also by George R. Nielsen:

The Kickapoo People. Phoenix, Arizona: Indian Tribal Series, 1975.

In Search of a Home: The Sorbs (Wends) on the Australian and Texas Frontiers. Birmingham, England: University of Birmingham, 1977.

The Danish Americans. Boston, Massachusetts: Twayne Press, 1981.

In Search of a Home: Nineteenth Century Wendish Migration. College Station, Texas: Texas A & M University Press, 1989.

Johann Kilian, Pastor: A Wendish Lutheran in Germany and Texas. Serbin, Texas: Texas Wendish Heritage Society, 2003.

(Co-author) *Walking George: The Life of George John Beto and the Rise of the Modern Texas Prison System*. Denton, Texas: University of North Texas Press, 2005.

Vengeance

in a

Small Town

The Thorndale Lynching of 1911

GEORGE R. NIELSEN

iUniverse, Inc.
Bloomington

Vengeance in a Small Town
The Thorndale Lynching of 1911

Copyright © 2011 by George R. Nielsen

iUniverse books may be ordered through booksellers or by contacting:
iUniverse
1663 Liberty Drive
Bloomington, IN 47403
www.iuniverse.com
1-800-Authors (1-800-288-4677)

ISBN: 978-1-4502-8796-8 (pbk)
ISBN: 978-1-4502-8797-5 (ebk)

Printed in the United States of America
iUniverse rev. date: 1/28/11

God made the country and man made the city, but the devil made the small town.

—George J. Beto and others.

Contents

Illustrations

Preface

Anyone who has grown up in a small town has learned two facts of life: people know who you are and word travels fast. Nothing, one would conclude, could be kept secret. Yet, paradoxically, small towns abound in secrets. Usually these secrets are about some major violation of the Ten Commandments or a disgrace to the family name. Older people do talk about these things, but they suddenly change the subject when little ears are seen approaching. Or, if anyone did ask, the usual standard response was, "Some things are better left unsaid."

I grew up in a small town, Thorndale, Texas, population 898. It was a typical small town with all the attendant advantages and liabilities. But Thorndale also had a secret that dwarfed all the other secrets—something about a murder and a lynching. On several occasions I heard that a lynching had taken place on the corner of Highway 79 and Main Street just in front of Moerbe's Mobile gas station. Other than hearing that a lynching had happened, I never learned any details. No one I knew ever said anything about it. I assumed that there was not much to it, just another Southern-style lynching widely practiced at that time in order to keep the black minority in its place. Much later I learned that the victim was not an African American, but a Mexican, and that it was not for social control, but for instant, albeit illegal, retribution.

Although many newspapers, including the *New York Times*, carried reports of the lynching, once the trials were concluded, the issue faded from the public press. National and world affairs such as World War I, the Depression, and World War II attracted attention. Even county and local histories written after the incident made no reference to the lynching. Instead the accounts were sanitized with extensive listings of churches, schools, and civic groups. Not until 1974, after the African American civil rights focus had widened and invigorated the Chicano movement, was the subject raised. José Limón, in an article tracing the origins of the Mexican American civil rights struggle, listed the Thorndale lynching as one of the sparks that ignited it.[1] Since then other books and articles have referred to the incident and their authors have repeated Limón's material without further research, and none has questioned the assumption that the Thorndale lynching was a racist act.

The purpose of this study is not to deny or to bemoan the existence of racism, bigotry, or lawlessness in our nation's history. They all existed, and there is no defense for a society that spawned lynching. But neither should every act involving a racial minority be viewed as a racist act. Carrigan and Webb[2] concluded that "racial prejudice was the primary force in fomenting mob violence against Mexicans." However, if we apply their statement to the Thorndale case, that would make us the hangmen of the lynchers. Thorndale in 1911, the year of the lynching, was a community that had not cut the threads connecting it to the earlier times and instead of condemning the citizens as racists, I would like to describe society as it existed in Thorndale's neighborhood one hundred years ago and how the lynching was a logical consequence. So neatly manicured were the neural pathways of those citizens that when the stimulus of a murder occurred, lynching was the immediate response, without any thought to either the act of retribution itself or to the race of the victim. White, black, or brown, none was exempt. A life for a life.[3]

At the same time while Thorndale was linked to its past, it was also making strides to enter the modern era. And that look to the future, which in Thorndale meant material wealth and such civic features as more brick stores, concrete sidewalks, and electricity, also required newer attitudes of justice and order that were not in harmony with previous practices. In the tug-of-war between the mindsets of the old and new centuries, Thorndale's old traditions momentarily prevailed and a lynching resulted.

Just as the press and local histories buried the event in the vault of the past, contemporary individuals could say, "Some things are better left unsaid." But after one hundred years it is time tell the story—as thoroughly and as accurately as possible. Our failures are as instructive as are our successes. On June 19, 1911, two lives were taken by good people in a community built on good will. Perhaps this history will help us understand how such an aberration could happen and also how this single incident influenced society far beyond the city limits.

Thorndale itself was not an actual victim of the lynching but the town changed as it moved further into the twentieth century. Beginning with the Great Depression Thorndale, like scores of small towns along the railroad, began its slow decline. Dirt roads and horses and buggies were replaced by paved roads and automobiles; and the agricultural economy, Thorndale's major resource, was weakened by economic hard times. Thorndale had seen its heyday, and although its business sector declined, after one hundred years the commercial block and the residential community cling to life.[4]

Steve's Cash Store occupies Thorndale's oldest brick building, built in 1902, Butt's Dry Goods, founded in 1932, continues to attract customers, and the Bank of Texas, current occupant of the Thorndale State Bank building with its polished brass, marble, and mahogany, still preserves the ambience of security and stability. Nevertheless, there are a few grassy lots where formerly a store stood, and antique shops now occupy some of the brick buildings that previously sheltered hardware stores and barbershops. The antiques, artifacts, and used furniture all serve as nostalgic symbols of Thorndale's past. And somewhere in that collection of old furniture, there is a wardrobe with a skeleton in it.

I acknowledge with gratitude certain individuals who have supported my efforts. Patricia Swayze Larsen first called my attention to on-line references of the lynching; Bill E. Biar, Roy H. Zieschang, and Weldon Mersiovsky supplied newspaper clippings, photos and other data; and Eleanor Eifert assisted with the translation of documents and newspapers written in Spanish. The gracious staffs at the University of Texas' Dolph Briscoe Center for American History and the Benson Latin American Center must be mentioned; as well as specific individuals such as Sergio Velasco, research assistant at the Texas State Archives and Alejandro Padilla Nieto and Jorge Fuentes at the Archivo Histórico Genaro Estrada in Mexico City. During the years of research the librarians at the Rapid City Library answered many of my requests for books through Interlibrary Loan, and I benefited from the resources of the Lucy Hill Patterson Library in Rockdale, Texas. Karen DeVinney provided invaluable editorial assistance. And finally, I must acknowledge Richard Maxwell Brown, of the University of Oregon, who influenced my thinking through a National Endowment for the Humanities seminar on violence in America.

Names and Terms

Gabriel Gamez—Father of the lynching victim. He signed his name as Gamez.

Antonio Gomez—Lynching victim and spelled as newspapers and documents spelled it.

Charles Zieschang—victim of the stabbing also know by his German name, Karl.

Mexican American or Tejano—Texas citizen of Mexican descent.

Mexican—Citizen of Mexico, person of Mexican descent whose citizenship is not known, or a group of Mexicans and Mexican Americans.

Anglo—White American generally in contrast to Mexican.

I. THE MURDER
AND LYNCHING

June nineteenth, the date of the murder and lynching, is also a significant date for African Americans in Texas. That is the date in 1865 when the Union officer, General Gordon Granger, in charge of the newly arrived army in Galveston, read a general order ending slavery in Texas. Ever since then "Juneteenth" has been a holiday for Texas blacks, and in recent years it has become a date to remember for all blacks in America.

The blacks in Milam County celebrated their day in 1911, but in Thorndale, nothing out of the ordinary took place, and for the white community, it was business as usual. During the heat of the day, outside activity slowed down and people looked for shade. The few shoppers preferred the western side of Main Street where the store fronts with the verandas offered the most shade against the afternoon sun. In "the evening" as the residents called the late afternoon, activity picked up and continued until twilight. On that day the sun set at 7:34.

At about seven o'clock, Charles Zieschang, owner of the Thorndale Garage, which was located on South First Street three doors off of Main Street, walked eastward toward the Old Bank Saloon, also known as the Bank Saloon. To his left, across the street, was the Thorndale Mercantile Company's building, the oldest brick commercial building in town, and to his right was a drug store. The Bank Saloon occupied the ground floor of the corner building, while part of the second floor housed the telephone switchboard, a real estate and insurance business, and a medical office. Earlier that day Zieschang had stood in front of the saloon between the

1

Lone Star Beer sign and a telephone pole and posed for a photograph. The photo must have been a spur-of-the-moment event because Zieschang wore his work clothes: a loose fitting shirt and trousers. And instead of the straw hat worn by farmers, Zieschang wore a workman's cap.

Charles Zieschang, 1911.
Photo taken on the day of his death at
the place where he was stabbed
Courtesy Roy H. Zieschang

As he approached the corner he stopped to talk with some men who were standing near the entrance. One was Constable Robert L. McCoy, age thirty-eight, single, and the owner of a livery stable. Another was William S. Stephens, Zieschang's close friend and owner of the saloon. And there were two local men, Johnny Davis and Wallace Young. As they were talking, Antonio Gomez, a fourteen-year-old Mexican lad, came walking along the sidewalk, whittling on a wood shingle and scattering the curls of wood on the walk. Stephens said to him, "Quit littering up the sidewalk, as fast as I clean it up, you mess it up again," and grabbed Antonio in a playful manner, scuffled around a little, and turned him loose. Antonio then backed off a bit and resumed his whittling.

Zieschang said, "I can make the damn little skunk quit whittling," and snatched the shingle out of Antonio's hand and took it with him into the saloon. The other men remained outside and discussed whose duty it was to keep the sidewalks clean. A few minutes later Zieschang came back out and said something to the effect that "If the son-of-a bitch did that in front of my store, I would paddle his ass with it." Antonio, about three steps away, lunged at him with his knife and struck him in the left breast below the collarbone.

Antonio pulled out the knife and threw it to the pavement. A bystander picked it up and said to Zieschang, "There is blood on the blade of the knife; that boy has stabbed you." Zieschang replied, "No, you are mistaken, he hasn't stabbed me." But then the blood began to gush from the artery above the heart where it had been severed. The constable grabbed the boy while the others took Zieschang to the adjacent drugstore and called for a physician.

When the physician arrived they took Zieschang to a room above the saloon, quite likely the physician's office, near the telephone switchboard. Nothing could be done to stop the hemorrhaging and Zieschang died in approximately twenty minutes, at about seven-thirty.

As Zieschang lay bleeding to death Constable McCoy took Antonio north along Main Street, crossed the railroad tracks and then across the Taylor to Rockdale road, known as N. Railroad Street, and locked the lad in the town calaboose. The calaboose could hardly be classified as a secure jail, but served more as holding pen for rowdy imbibers. While McCoy was locking up Gomez, word of the incident spread across town, and soon Main Street and the side street were filled with townsfolk waiting for word of Zieschang's condition. When McCoy returned to the crime scene he sent word to all five of Thorndale's saloons to close their doors and they remained closed for the night.

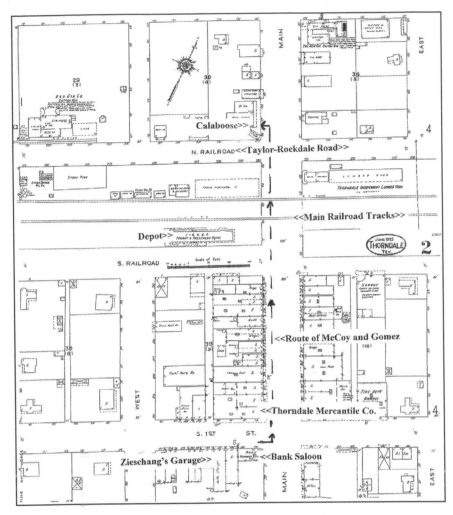

Route taken by McCoy and Gomez from
the Bank Saloon to the calaboose.

When Zieschang's death was announced, the crowd, estimated to number between one and two hundred, became agitated and there were words of violence and cursing. McCoy, when he heard the announcement of Zieschang's death and sensed the anger in the crowd, left for his home to pick up his coat and gun. Thirty minutes later at about eight o'clock he arrived at the calaboose where approximately forty men had gathered. He unlocked the door, took out the lad and locked a small trace chain around his neck. Wilford Wilson, one of the men near the calaboose, offered to help McCoy. As the two men left the calaboose area with their prisoner, McCoy told the men not to follow them. They did not follow.

The Lynching

While the details surrounding Zieschang's death have been well documented by several witnesses, the events that followed and eventually led to Gomez's death are not as coherently described. One reason could be the crisis nature of the events, and another was that the events that unfolded from eight-thirty to ten took place in the dark. There were no electric street lights, there was no moon, and in the deep twilight people were shadows.

The following narrative is based on the testimony given at the court of inquiry that followed the inquest. After the witnesses had been questioned, the court summarized each witness's testimony and the witness signed the document. The document that survived is therefore a collection of summary statements and not the series of questions and answers.[5] Details that might have given us a better picture of the events could have been excluded. To compensate for the possible omissions, information from other sources has been added to the following account so long as the information was consistent with the official testimony. Although these testimonies became the basis for the later trials, testimony given later at the trials was not always consistent with the testimony given at the court of inquiry. Contradictions that appeared between witnesses at the court of inquiry as well as contradictions between statements given at the jury trial and at the court of inquiry are included in brackets.

When McCoy and Wilson, with Gomez in tow, left the calaboose, they headed west toward the Thorndale Gin Company, a cotton gin about one hundred yards away. The gin, McCoy thought, would be a good place to hide Gomez from the irate citizens until he obtained a conveyance and transported the boy to Cameron, twenty-three miles away, and the protection of the county jail. McCoy asked Wilson to go to E. A. Johnson, who happened to be Zieschang's business partner, to supply an automobile. [McCoy said the three went to the gin house, but Wilson testified the three went about twenty-five steps from the calaboose and he then left for the car.] McCoy stayed at the gin house a short time and then took Gomez to the home of G. W. Penny and waited. Wilson was gone for more than an hour, and then appeared at the Penny house. [Nothing is stated how Wilson knew that McCoy had abandoned the gin and had gone to Penny's house.] Wilson had not been successful in his quest for the car because he never found Johnson and supposedly had waited for fifty minutes for Johnson to return. [McCoy testified that Johnson refused to provide the service.] When Wilson arrived at the Penny house, he found McCoy, Gomez, Penny, Penny's son, and an eighteen-year-old grandson there waiting. (The time would have been about nine-fifteen.) McCoy then left Wilson in charge of the prisoner while he tried to obtain a conveyance. He instructed Wilson to stand off a mob, if one appeared, until he returned, or to persuade Penny to engage them in conversation so Wilson could exit the back door of the house with the prisoner.

No sooner had McCoy departed than a group of men and boys appeared at Penny's front gate but did not enter the yard. Penny said there were four or five, and Wilson said there were four men at the gate and two farther back. Wilson could not see their faces, but recognized their voices. The men at Penny's gate claimed that they knew Penny was sheltering the lad and demanded that Penny turn him over. Wilson replied that McCoy had taken the boy away, but Penny, instead of supporting the deception about Gomez's presence, admitted that Gomez was in the house and that he would be protected. Penny told them to leave, and they went about thirty steps toward town. After the group had gone, Penny told Wilson that McCoy would meet him at the oil mill and that he and Gomez could leave through the back door of the house and make their way down the alley.

As Wilson and Gomez reached the alley, Wilson saw a person near the back gate but could not identify him. He and Gomez ran eastward down the alley about a hundred yards when he was met by a man on horseback and three men on foot. The men on foot tried to grab Gomez but Gomez at first avoided them by running around Wilson using him as a shield. Then, however, the horseman forced his horse between Wilson and Gomez, grabbed the chain and galloped eastward down the street dragging the boy. The three others ran after the horseman. [McCoy testified that the day after the lynching Wilson told him that twelve to fifteen men had taken Gomez away.] Wilson went south intending to go to town to get assistance. Before he got to town, he encountered the same four with a ladder at the telephone pole about eighty [two hundred] feet north of the depot, on the northwest corner of Main Street and the Taylor-Rockdale Road. Gomez had been suspended to a round of the ladder that was leaning against the telephone pole. The chain came loose from the ladder and Gomez dropped to the ground. Wilson rushed up to see if he could do something for the victim and saw one of the four men, Ezra Stephens, the son of the Bank Saloon's owner, kick the victim's head. Just at that moment the Rev. J. L. Watson, E. A. Johnson, and Buck Bonds, en route to their homes, came on to the scene. Watson testified that he saw Gomez, although unconscious, alive and gasping for air. [Bonds and Johnson agreed that Gomez was still alive but Wilson testified he was dead.] None of the four attempted to intervene.

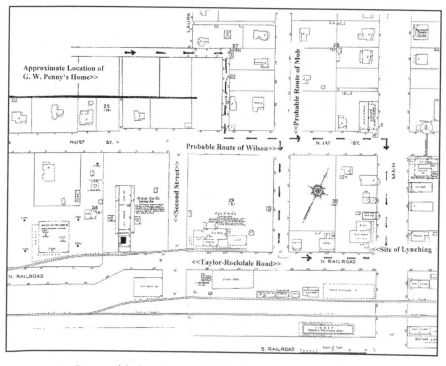

Routes likely taken by Wilford Wilson and the mob
from G. W. Penny's house to the site of the lynching.

Instead they went back to town. Wilson went to Woodbury Norris, the Justice of the Peace, and reported the events. He identified Ezra Stephens as the man on horseback and the three men on foot as Z. T. Gore, Jr., Garrett Noack, and Harry Wuensche. The three homeward bound men,

Watson, Bonds, and Johnson, gave no report, but returned to the street in front of the Bank Saloon where the crowd was still milling about. At the court of inquiry Bonds testified that he saw four or five men around Gomez and that Wilson was holding the chain. Watson testified that he saw six or seven men around Gomez, but he recognized only Wilson and Stephens and that Stephens twice kicked Gomez's head. E. A. Johnson saw ten to fifteen men. He did not see Gore in the group, but based on size and form, identified Ezra Stephens and Harry Wuensche. He also named T. J. Dube as a member of the group, a person no one else mentioned.

Constable McCoy, searching for a conveyance, learned of Gomez's death about twenty-five or thirty minutes after he had left Penny's house. Gus Williamson was the informant and the time would have been about nine-fifty-five. Within minutes of receiving the information, McCoy, along with Norris and two others, arrived at the crime scene, which by that time was deserted. McCoy lifted the body up and unfastened the trace chain. The body would have been removed around ten o'clock. Watson, Johnson, and Bonds, after joining the crowd at the Bank Saloon for about fifteen minutes, again headed home sometime between ten and ten-thirty, and saw the body suspended.

This is a summary of events with approximate times:

7:10 Stabbing on sidewalk

7:30 Zieschang's death

7:30–8:00 McCoy goes to his house for his gun and coat

8:00 McCoy removes Gomez from calaboose

8:15–9:15 Wilson attempts to obtain an automobile

McCoy takes Gomez to the gin and then to Penny's house

9:15 Wilson goes to Penny's house

9:20–9:45 McCoy searches for a conveyance

9:25 Four or five men gather at Penny's house

9:35 Wilson takes Gomez into alley

9:40 Seizure of Gomez

9:45 Lynching. Watson, Johnson, Bonds, and Wilson arrive at the scene

9:50 The witnesses go to town

9:55 McCoy learns of lynching

10:00 The body is removed.

Selected Newspaper Reports

The following newspaper reports illustrate how journalists handled the tragedy. The most detailed and most accurate was in the *Thorndale Thorn* because the editor could interview citizens and had three days to develop his report. The *San Antonio Express* appeared the day after the event and shows how the reporter took sketchy information and embellished it with details from previous lynchings. The *New York Times* tailored the story with a diplomatic slant; *La Crónica* from Laredo articulated the Mexican point of view; and the *Giddings Deutsches Volksblatt* spoke for the Germans.

Report from the *Thorndale Thorn*, June 23, 1911

A DEPLORABLE TRAGEDY

THE STABBING AND KILLING OF A THORNDALE CITIZEN, FOLLOWED BY LYNCHING MURDERER

Thorndale was thrown into a furor of excitement about 7 o'clock Monday evening, June 19th, when the information was circulated that Charley Zieschang owner of the Thorndale Garage, had been stabbed by a Mexican lad and was dying.

The details of the murder, and the lynching of the lad are, as near as can be obtained, as follows: Shortly before 7 o'clock the Mexican lad was standing on the sidewalk in front of the Bank Saloon whittling on a small piece of board. Several citizens were also standing near and the lad was asked to stop whittling and the making of a litter on the walk. The lad replied with a oath that he would do as he pleased. One or two of the party then made some remarks to the lad in a jocular manner and Zieschang took the piece of board from him remarking that he would paddle him with it. Zieschang then stepped into the saloon, reappearing

9

in a few minutes stepped up to the crowd standing on the walk, and just as he stopped the Mexican lad stepped up to him and plunged his knife into his left breast just below the collar bone. The point of the knife ranged downward, severed an artery and entered the lung cavity. Zieschang was taken into the drug store next door and medical attention summoned. Upon the arrival of a physician he was removed to a room upstairs in the saloon building where he expired in a few minutes, or about twenty minutes after he received the wound.

Constable R. L. McCoy was standing within a few feet of the lad when he did the stabbing and immediately took charge of him locking him in the calaboose. As the crowd began to increase and it was announced that Zieschang was dead excitement increased and expressions of violence began to be passed through the crowd, which by this time had grown to one or two hundred. Constable McCoy fearing violence went to the calaboose and taking the lad out turned him over to Wilford Wilson who was to take him into hiding. Efforts were made to get an auto from Taylor and from San Gabriel to take his lad to Cameron, and information to the effect that this had been done was circulated among the infuriated crowd.

Mr. Wilson took the lad to the home of G. W. Penny where shortly after 9 o'clock they were located by a mob who demanded the prisoner. Mr. Wilson took the prisoner and went out the rear of the house around the barn and while in the alley at the Union Cotton Yard someone ran up to him on a horse and jerking the chain from him started towards the business portion of the town with the prisoner. The party of the horse was joined by the remainder of the mob as he entered the street and the prisoner was brought on down to Main street and hanged to the round of a tall ladder which was leaning against a telephone pole about two hundred feet north of the railroad crossing. He was hanged with the chain which had been placed around his neck when he was taken out into hiding. When it was announced that Zieschang was dead and threats of violence [about five words illegible] from the rapidly growing crowd the saloons of the town, five in number, all voluntarily closed their doors and remained closed during the night.

The lad was known here as Antonio Gomez and lived with his father, Gabriel Gomez, who has a large family and has been here several months contracting grubbing land. His age is placed at from fourteen to eighteen years.

So quiet and orderly was the work of the mob that the crowd of a hundred or two down on Main street not a block away knew nothing of what was going on, and the discovery of the lynching was made by parties who had left the crowd to go home supposing that everything had quieted down and that the prisoner was on his way to the county jail at Cameron.

Mr. Zieschang was twenty-six years of age and was born and reared in Williamson county about nine miles southwest of Thorndale and was a son of Mr. and Mrs. John Zieschang of the Noack community. He was married about six years ago to Miss Annie Moerbe, daughter of Mr. and Mrs. John Moerbe who live out just west of Thorndale. He is survived by his wife and three [four] small children besides his father and mother and several brothers and sisters and other relatives. He moved to Thorndale some two years or more ago and opened the Thorndale Garage which he has since conducted. His remains were interred in Saint Paul's Lutheran Cemetery at 4 o'clock Wednesday afternoon in the presence of one of the largest concourses ever assembled in that city of the dead, Rev. A. W. Kramer conducting the funeral obsequies. His tragic and untimely death is deeply regretted by the entire community and all join in extending condolence to the bereaved wife, little ones and relatives.

Report from the *San Antonio Express*, June 20, 1911

[Inaccurate information is in italics.]

THORNDALE MOB LYNCHES BOY WITH TRACE CHAINS

VENGEANCE QUICKLY EXECUTED ON MEXICAN LAD WHO KILLS PROMINENT CITIZEN

TELEPHONE POLE GALLOWS

LOCAL JAIL STORMED AFTER TRAGEDY CAUSED BY WHITTLING—*MEXICAN WATERMELON WAGON STOPPED AND TRACES USED AS A HANGMAN'S ROPE.*

Special Telegram to The Express

Thorndale, Tex., June 19—Charles Zeitung, [Zieschang] owner of the Thorndale garage and a member of a prominent family in this part of Milam County, was killed here at 7:30 o'clock this evening by an unknown *eighteen-year-old* Mexican boy. An hour and a half later the boy was taken from the *town jail by a mob of 100 citizens and hung to a telephone pole* in the main street.

After the body had swung in the public street *for an hour* it was taken down and *turned over to the Mexican colony*. There is much excitement in Thorndale tonight and Sheriff Allen Hooks, who lives in Cameron, is reported on his way here *with a posse.*

Zietung was 28 years old, married and had four children. He was popular in this township and has a number of relatives living in this vicinity.

WHITTLING LEADS TO TRAGEDY

The young Mexican was sitting on the sidewalk *in front of Zeitung's garage* whittling a *stick* with a pocket knife when Zeitung ordered him to cease making a litter. The boy, according to bystanders, got angry and stabbed Zeitung in the heart. The man died *instantly.* McCoy, constable of the precinct was within a few feet of the knifing [smudged] arrested the boy, lodged him in the town jail *on the charge of murder*, and went away leaving him *in the custody of the jailor.* As Thorndale is not the county seat there is no county jail here and the local place of detention is a flimsy thing. The killing caused intense excitement and shortly after dark Zeitung's friends began to gather in the streets. The town has a population of about 1000 and practically every man was in the streets within an hour of the killing and there were shouts of "Lynch him."

Word got around that Sheriff Hooks was on his way from Cameron *with a posse of men to take charge of the Mexican. No sooner had this been verified than a mob of at least one hundred citizens, including men prominent in the county, formed in a mass and, proceeding to the jail, broke down the door and hustled the frightened youth to a telephone pole* a block from the railroad station.

Twenty men ran for ropes, but the mob was too impatient to wait. Men held up a Mexican who was driving a load of watermelons, unhitched his team and fastened the four trace chains together.

LYNCHED FROM POLE WITH CHAIN

The chain was fastened about the boy's neck and an end was fixed in the belt of a youth. *A dozen hands boosted the lad up the pole and he passed the chain over the arm that holds the wires.* Dozens of hands grasped the chain and the Mexican, his hands tied behind him, was *lifted six feet* from the ground and *the chain made fast to a foot spike in the pole.*

The lynching was on the main street and the body was allowed to hang there *for an hour* within view of every man, woman and child in the town.

The mob dispersed and ten minutes after the hanging not a man in town would acknowledge he had been in the neighborhood at the time. Accordingly, no one can be found who will tell whether the Mexican made a statement why he stabbed Zietung.

The majority of the mob are men well known in Milam County, some known throughout the State.

The name of the Mexican cannot be ascertained tonight. The people who took the body say he had lived here about nine months and they know no reason for the killing.

Report from the *New York Times,* June 26, 1911

LYNCHING ANGERS MEXICO

WASHINGTON TO TAKE UP THE HANGING OF A MEXICAN BOY IN TEXAS

Galveston, Texas, June 25. The Mexican Government is not satisfied with the report of Consul Diebold, giving the result of his investigation into the lynching of Antonio Gomez, the fourteen-year-old Mexican, by a mob at Thorndale, Texas. Four men arrested say they took the boy from the house where the constable left him to protect him from the mob.

Reports said that one hundred men participated in the lynching. The Mexican Government representatives profess to have evidence from witnesses, whose names they are willing to furnish, against at least twenty-five citizens of Milam County, and demands that they be arrested and punished. Two witnesses are under the protection of the Mexican Consul, having been threatened with death if they testify against any Thorndale citizens.

The Mexican Government condemns what it calls the lack of justice and effort on the part of Texas peace officers and the citizens in punishing the guilty persons. The Texas State officials, having failed to produce evidence pointing to the leaders of the mob, the matter is to be referred to Washington.

Report from [Laredo] *La Crónica*, July 13, 1911

El Lynchamiento infame de un niño de tiernos años por una turba de alemanes, en Thorndale, Condado de Milan [*sic*], Texas, es el acto criminal mas negro, más corbarde é infame que jamas haya manchado las páginas de la historic del Estado de Texas. Los criminales mas desalmados nunca han revelado tanta cobardía alma mas negra é instintos feroces mas atroces.

…El aleman tan querido y tan respetados de todo mexicano, ha sentido ya los primeros sintómas de la venganza. Muchos mexicanos han protestado no comprar en los establecimientos alemanes de México, en tanto que no se imponga el castigo que merecen los barbaros lynchadores de Thorndale.

[Translation] The infamous lynching of a young boy by the hand of Germans in Thorndale, Milam County, is the blackest, most cowardly and infamous criminal act that has ever soiled the history of the State of Texas. These criminals had never shown such cowardice, such black souls, and such savage instincts.

…The Germans that are well loved and respected by all the Mexicans are feeling already the first symptoms of vengeance. A lot of Mexicans are protesting by not buying in German stores in Mexico, as long as the barbarian lynchers of Thorndale are not punished.

Report from *Giddings Deutsches Volksblatt*, June 22, 1911

Wieder wurde uns ein Trauer- und Unglücksfall berichtet, welcher sich an Montagnachmittag in Thorndale zutrug. Es wurde dort nämlich Herr

Karl Zieschang jr. Sohnen des Herrn John Zieschang von Hochkirch von einem Mexikaner menchlings erstochen. Mit dem noch unmündigen Mörder, dessen man habhaft wurde, machte man kurzen Prozess, indem man denselben dem Constable entriss u. sofort aufknüpfte. Genauere Einzelheiten über den Vorfall stehen uns leider nicht zur Verfügung.

[Translation] Once again we have received a sad and tragic notice of an event, which in this instance, took place Monday afternoon in Thorndale. There, Mr. Karl Zieschang, Jr., son of Mr. John Zieschang of Hochkirch, was stabbed by a Mexican youth. The under-aged murdered was apprehended and given quick justice, in that he was torn from the constable and immediately hanged. More specific details of this incident are not available.

II. EUROPEAN SETTLEMENT OF MILAM AND WILLIAMSON COUNTIES

Even though Thorndale is situated in Milam County, its history is linked almost as much to neighboring Williamson County as it is to Milam County. Located within one mile of the Williamson County line, Thorndale's economic and social life was largely oblivious of the political line that separated the two counties. To understand Thorndale's development it is therefore necessary to look also at Williamson County and to fit both counties into the region that gave Thorndale its sustenance.

The first settlement of Europeans in the general area was in 1748 when Franciscan missionaries founded a mission near the confluence of Brushy Creek and the San Gabriel River, approximately twelve miles from contemporary Thorndale. Two more missions in proximity to the first followed in 1749. The missions were a collaborative effort between the missionaries and the viceroy in Mexico City who represented the Spanish government. While the missionaries were interested in Christianizing the Indians and teaching them European ways, the government hoped the missions would counteract the French influence seeping into Texas from Louisiana. Without the viceroy's authorization, the missions would not have been founded. The viceroy paid the salaries of the missionaries and also sent a small contingent of soldiers to protect the mission and its friendly Bidai, Coco, and Tonkawa wards from the marauding tribes. The site, however, was less than satisfactory, and coupled with the imprudent actions of some of the military personnel, controversy resulted in their subsequent closing in1755, seven years after their founding.[6]

Although the locations of the missions are known as a result of archeological excavations, there are no crumbling walls to testify to their existence. A University of Texas historian, Herbert E. Bolton, conducted research in the area in 1907 and since then there have been subsequent archeological studies revealing burial sites, beads, pieces of glass bottles, and irrigation ditches.[7]

One "artifact" that also testified to the Spanish presence and one that remained for decades, was a living one: cattle. Cattle were synonymous with Spanish expansion in the American Southwest. Men not only used oxen to pull the wagons and draw the plows, but cattle were the mobile commissary that provided meat for explorers and for the missions that followed. Every twelve or fifteen days, for example, the missionaries slaughtered an animal and distributed the meat to the Indians. Invariably, during the seven years, some of the cattle escaped or wandered away and began reproducing in the hospitable environment.[8]

France ceased being a competitor for Texas in 1762 when, as a result of European wars and diplomatic agreements, France transferred its claim on Louisiana to Spain. That transfer calmed Spanish fears of losing influence in Texas for a time, but the calm was short-lived. In 1800 the French, under Napoleon, regained control of Louisiana. At that time, Napoleon needed Louisiana to anchor his project of creating a French empire in the Americas. His dreams, however, were not realistic and so he pursued projects elsewhere and sold Louisiana to the United States in 1803.

The United States was as great a threat to Spanish Texas as France had been, so Spain once more became concerned about foreign intrusion. The boundaries separating Louisiana and Texas had never been clearly fixed, and during the purchase negotiations when American diplomats tried to pin down the details, Napoleon's foreign minister brushed the question aside and suggested that the Americans "make the most of it." Some Americans, such as President Thomas Jefferson, argued that Texas was included in the purchase.[9]

Spanish officials disagreed and asked José Antonio Pichardo to trace the history of Europeans in Texas and show that Texas belonged to Spain instead of France and therefore was not part of the Louisiana Purchase.

Pichardo's report, based on research and travel, not only provided the documentation, but also included comments about the vacant lands and their potential for development. His tour of Texas brought him to the site of the deserted Spanish missions in the Brushy Creek-San Gabriel area and he commented about the "incredible number of cattle" present in the district, and those cattle, he concluded, could provide the foundation of a settlement.[10]

The problem of drawing a specific boundary line between the United States and Spain's Mexico went unresolved for sixteen years and Texas was left wide open to political intrigue and filibustering expeditions. Finally, in 1819, Spain and the United States signed the Adams-Onís Treaty in which the United States gained concessions in the Pacific Northwest, but yielded its claim to Texas and agreed to a clearly delineated boundary between Louisiana Territory and Texas. The treaty again removed a foreign threat and consequently Spain's officials in Mexico lost the incentive for strengthening Spain's presence in Texas with government-sponsored settlements. The region once more belonged to the wild cattle.

Settlement, nevertheless, was viewed as desirable, and when Moses Austin requested permission to bring in settlers to Texas under Spain's empresarial system, he was welcomed. Implementation of any colonization efforts, however, would not be carried out by Moses Austin but by his son, Stephen; and the land would not be distributed by Spain, but by its descendant, Mexico, having gained its independence in 1821. Land became the inducement for populating Texas. The *empresarios*, Stephen F. Austin and others, received extensive tracts of land in return for recruiting settlers, surveying the land, and maintaining law and order. Settlers, in turn, received smaller plots of land and they were required to pay the *empresario* twelve and one-half cents for each acre.

Anglo American Texas

Contemporary Milam and Williamson counties were part of a block of land first assigned by Mexico to Robert Leftwich of Nashville, Tennessee. But there was no settlement and the contract changed hands. Finally, in 1834, under the leadership of Sterling C. Robertson, settlement began around his center of operations, which he called Nashville-on-the-Brazos.

Two years earlier, in October 1832, the Mexican government, hoping to tighten administrative control of the region, had divided Texas into large administrative units called municipalities. Nashville-on-the-Brazos and what later became Milam County were located within one of these areas named the Municipality of Viesca. During the Texas Revolution, in November 1835, the Texans changed the name to the Municipality of Milam, in honor of Benjamin Milam who had been killed at San Antonio in the opening days of the rebellion. The next year, 1836, the Texas Republic's Congress reorganized the municipalities into counties and the Municipality of Milam became Milam County. So large was the area that eventually thirty-four Texas counties, including the contemporary Milam and Williamson, were completely or partially carved from it.[11]

Although Sarahville, located at the falls of the Brazos, had been designated as the county seat, Indian threats dissuaded settlers from traveling to Sarahville and instead they went to the more secure Nashville, which served as the de facto administrative center. Later Caldwell also served as the county seat and alternated with Nashville. Finally, in 1846 the political leaders named Cameron the county seat of Milam County.[12]

As the American population spread farther westward, the settlers complained about the distance they needed to travel to transact business at Cameron, so 107 citizens petitioned state officials for the creation of a separate county. The Texas Legislature honored the request with a law passed on March 13, 1848, and named the new county Williamson after Robert "Three-legged Willie" Williamson, another one of the leaders of the Texas Republic. The legislature also selected Georgetown as the county seat.[13] Both of the modern counties, Williamson, and what was left of Milam, were each about a thousand square miles in size. In 1850 the population of Milam County was 2,907 and Williamson County was 1,534.

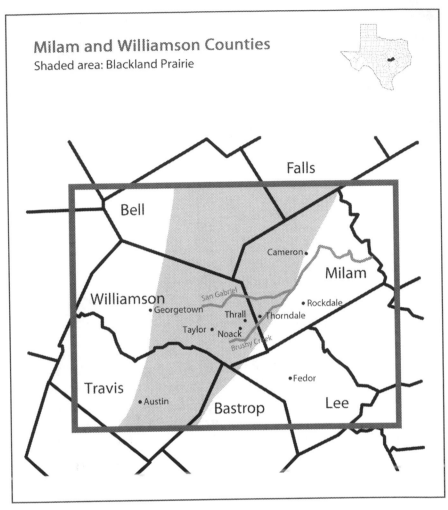

Map of Milam and Williamson counties.

The vegetation of the eastern and southern portion of the newly diminished Milam County, approximately three-fifths of the county, belonged to the post oak savannah region supporting oaks and tall grasses. Land with timber, not grassland, attracted the frontiersman, and it, not the prairie, was occupied first. Timber was both a bane and a blessing. Before fields could be cultivated the trees had to be cut and the land cleared. But with trees the pioneers could build cabins and fences and use the wood to make their fires. Subsistence agriculture was the primary economic activity from early in the county's history until the 1870s.

One of the early pioneers, Noah Smithwick, settled on Brushy Creek in 1850, up stream from the missions. Offspring of the Spanish mission cattle roamed the countryside and Smithwick hoped to make a living from those cattle. His efforts failed and he moved on to other ventures, but he did identify the location of the missions as approximately ten miles from the confluence of the Brushy with the San Gabriel. He could see a mound, the remains of an adobe building, but he also reported that "goodly trees" were reclaiming the terrain.[14]

Subsistence agriculture, as practiced in the early days of Milam and Williamson counties, operated on the idea that the farmer produced almost everything he consumed. The mainstays of subsistence farming were corn, wheat, sweet potatoes, cattle, both for beef and for milk, and hogs, as well as fruit and vegetables from the garden.[15] Security meant a full smokehouse, cellar, and granary. The settlers sold and traded the small surpluses for such items such as coffee and salt, and used any currency for the payment of debts and taxes.

Most of the early settlers of Milam County originated from other Southern states and many brought slaves with them. During the 1850s cotton production grew, so that by 1860 Milam farmers produced 2,238 bales. And as cotton production increased, so did the number of slaves. In 1850 there were 436 slaves in a total population of 2,907 and by 1860 there were 1,542 slaves in a free population of 3,633. By the start of the Civil War slaves constituted about 30 percent of Milam's population, close to the average for the state.[16] Early Milam County fit firmly into the Southern tradition and on the question of secession its voters soundly endorsed exiting the Union by a 468 to 135 vote.

The remaining part of Milam County, the western and northern part, was not wooded. The area was part of the Central Prairie, a wedge of fertile land four hundred miles long, which extended from San Antonio through Austin and Dallas, all the way to Red River. The Central Prairie, in turn, was divided into the Blackland Prairie and the Grand Prairie, and the Blackland Prairie with its fertile soil became the trading region for Thorndale.[17] Grass predominated, and any trees, mesquite, live oak, or pecan, were largely restricted to isolated clumps or to the drainage system of the San Gabriel River in the northern part, or to its tributary, Brushy Creek, in the southern part. So the early pioneers planted their agricultural settlements along the streams in order to utilize the timber and, like the settlers of the post oak savannah, practiced subsistence agriculture. Intensive agricultural development would not take place until the time of the railroad and the introduction of the barbed wire fence.

When the political division of Milam and Williamson counties had been drawn, space and distance were the deciding factors and not natural barriers or vegetation. Soil and vegetation on either side of the line that divided Milam and Williamson counties were similar. Williamson County was almost a mirror image of Milam County. It also was divided into two parts. Williamson's eastern portion, with the Blackland Prairie, reflected Milam's western half, and Williamson's western part, like Milam's eastern part, was wooded. However, Williamson's western half, on the other side of the Balcones Escarpment, was higher, drier, and hillier than the eastern half of Milam. And the vegetation was brush instead of savannah.[18]

The Williamson County census of 1850, taken two years after its creation, listed a population of 1,379 whites and 155 Negro slaves.[19] Most of the settlers were also from Southern states, which explains the presence of slaves, although a number of settlers originated from Illinois. In the decade from 1850 to1860 the population increased to 3,638 whites and 891 slaves, with slaves constituting about 20 percent of the population. In contrast to Milam County, which overwhelmingly approved of secession, Williamson County included more unionists and the vote against secession was 480 to 347.

Williamson County agriculture was also subsistence farming and included crops similar to those of Milam County. But in addition to farming, settlers raised cattle on the unfenced prairie. It was profitable and the number of beef cattle in Williamson County tripled from 11,973 head in 1850 to 38,114 in 1860. Some profits resulted from producing salted beef or driving cattle to buyers in New Orleans, but the primary value lay in the production of hides and tallow.

The hide and tallow trade is usually identified in the popular mind as a California activity. The demand for hides by the Boston leather producers and for candles by the miners in South America resulted in the venture utilizing sailing ships that carried these products from the west coast of North American to its east coast through the straits off Cape Horn. Richard Henry Dana, Jr., who made the voyage himself from 1834 to

1836, popularized the activity in *Two Years before the Mast*. Texas cattle were closer to Boston than those of California, but at the time Dana was on the voyage, the Texans were fighting for independence. A few hide and tallow factories began to process Texas cattle in the days of the Texas Republic but the industry did not mature until after the Mexican War in 1848, and then, all along the Gulf Coast from Galveston to Corpus Christi, where streams enabled ships to approach land, processing plants accepted cattle. Cattlemen herded their wild cattle from the interior to the coast where the hide, tallow, bones, and horns were collected and the remains discharged into the rivers. Fish came to feed on the remains and grew to legendary size.

As cattlemen pushed farther inland and driving the cattle to the coast became impractical, they established their own rendering operations away from the coast. One of these rendering plants was located on Brushy Creek in Williamson County.[20] Many cattlemen, even without the income from tallow, were satisfied with profits from only the hides. Hides were sufficiently valuable so that a law was passed that anyone who came across a dead cow could skin the animal and sell the hide no matter whose brand it carried. On the unfenced range the cattle drifted and during winter die offs, the law made sense. But it opened the door for conflict as it provided cover for thieves to shoot branded cattle and claim that the animal had been found dead.[21]

The Civil War interrupted the hide and tallow trade, but in 1865, after the war's conclusion, it resumed on a reduced scale and continued until the mid-1870s.[22] The loss of income as a result of declining hide sales was more than offset by a new and insatiable demand for beef by workers in the Northern manufacturing cities. The landscape of the cattle business changed. Instead of herding the cattle south toward the ports on the Gulf of Mexico, the cattlemen headed them north to the nearest railroad stations in Missouri and Kansas.

During the Civil War the unattended cattle had reproduced by astounding numbers and at war's end an animal in Texas sold for as little as $5.00. That same animal was worth $30 in the North and the mathematics of profit persuaded ambitious men to enter the business. Because the grazing land in Texas was open range and wild unbranded cattle roamed those ranges, start-up costs for cattle operations were minimal. It was largely a matter of branding the wild cattle and leaving them alone until the annual round-up. There the calves were branded with the same brand as the mother cow and cattle were grouped to form a herd for the long drive north, Williamson County lay astride several feeder trails of the well-known Chisholm Trail. In the fifteen years between 1866 and 1880, more than four million head of cattle left the state.

The money brought back by the drovers set Texas apart from other Southern states. The war had disrupted the Southern transportation and economic systems, and the Southern agricultural economy, based largely on cotton, was slow to recover. Texas not only escaped extensive damage from battles, it had a commodity other than cotton that infused cash into the state.

One of the pioneer families in the southern part of Williamson County was that of James Olive, his wife, and six sons. The family had migrated from Mississippi to Texas in 1843. Olive selected land midway between Yegua (YEAH-wah) Creek and Brushy Creek and made his living with the hide and tallow trade. Because of his early participation in the business he was well situated to take advantage of the new opportunities of herding cattle north.[23]

James Olive's first son, Isom Prentice, or "Print," had been an infant during the trek to Texas and as he grew older the life of cattle and horses became his own. In 1861 that life was interrupted by the Civil War and he enlisted and fought for the Confederacy. After the war Print returned to Williamson County to resume his livelihood, and soon took over the leadership of the family enterprise. In 1866, for example, he managed a round-up for the entire region and later participated in cattle drives to Abilene and Ellsworth, Kansas. In 1869 he helped drive 2,000 cattle to Fort Kearny, Nebraska. With the assistance of three brothers, Thomas, Ira, and Bob, Print quickly became one of the big cattle ranchers in Williamson County.[24]

Although Milam and Williamson counties were generally identical, there were subtle differences. Of the two counties Milam had incorporated a stronger Southern heritage. Milam had supported secession while Williamson had a northern element that identified with the Union. In Milam County, in 1870, thirty out of every one hundred persons was black, while in Williamson it was twenty out of every hundred. The economy of Milam in 1870 was a subsistence economy of corn and hogs, and some cotton, which reflected the Southern heritage, while Williamson's economy, though it also included subsistence farming, profited from cattle and assumed more of a Western orientation. So even though Thorndale was located in Milam County, its economic ties to Williamson County influenced its cultural development. Thorndale inherited traits from both the Southern and the Western traditions.

The Railroad Era

From the time of the Civil War to the era of the automobile, the railroad was the engine of growth in Texas. Unhindered by rainfall or the dark of night, the railroad connected the isolated spaces of the state to the settled areas. The dilemma for railroad construction, however, was the question of which comes first, the railroad or the customer. To return a profit the railroad needed things to transport, but until a railroad was built, farmers could not occupy the land and produce sufficient materials for the railroad to ship. Railroad construction needed to go first and acceptable profits would be delayed. To avoid placing all the risk on the corporation and to stimulate construction, the taxpayers, through their governments, provided some incentives. Even with governmental aid, however, railroads were plagued with bankruptcies and struggled for stability through receiverships and consolidation.

One form of subsidizing railroad companies was through grants of public land. This type of support was an option for Texas because Texas had retained its lands when it became a state. The advantage for using land grants was that it cost the state nothing and there was no need to raise taxes. The railroad in turn could benefit by forming a land company and generating cash by selling the land to prospective settlers. However, the state's constitution, ratified in 1869 during Reconstruction, prohibited granting land to railroads. Instead, the constitution authorized an alternative type of support in the form of bonds. The bonds enabled the railroad to gather funds for track construction and the railroads would eventually redeem them; but in the meantime, the state paid the interest on the bonds and those payments came from increased taxes. A third form of subsidy was exempting the railroad from state taxes. Exemption did not entail an actual increase in taxes but it did deprive the state of potential revenue.[25]

After the Civil War, the Texas government, under the leadership of the Republicans, eagerly addressed the task of railroad development. At the war's end, the big sprawling state could claim only 341 miles of railroad. So while American citizens watched crews building the northern transcontinental railroads, Texas Republicans embraced railroad construction as the cornerstone of their economic policy. The minority Democrats, even while attacking nearly every program proposed by the Republicans, wholeheartedly endorsed railroad expansion. The result was progress, and by 1870 Texas had 711 miles of track and by 1873 there were 1,600 miles.[26]

One of the first railroads chartered after the war, in 1866, was the Houston and Great Northern. The backers of the railroad were Texans, including William Marsh Rice and W. J. Hutchins, and one of its general managers was Thomas Campbell, a future governor of the state. The 1869 Constitution, which sheltered public lands, had not been ratified, so granting public lands was still an option. State support was generous and the company not only received twenty sections of lands for each mile of track it laid, it also was granted exemption from state taxes for twenty-five years. Construction finally began in 1870 and by May 1873 it operated 252 miles of track from Houston to Palestine.[27]

Historians of the first transcontinental railroad, completed in 1869 at Promontory Point, Utah, tell the story of Chinese workers laboring on the Central Pacific and European immigrants doing the work on the Union Pacific. The laborers for Texas railroads often were convicts. The Huntsville penitentiary had accepted its first inmate in 1849. In order to keep penitentiary costs to a minimum and avoid the need for raising taxes, prisoners were required to work. In 1871, in an attempt to further maximize income and minimize expense, the state entered into a fifteen-year lease agreement with the Galveston firm of Ward, Dewey, and Company. The actual prison was to be managed by the company and the expenses would be recouped from prisoner labor. Some of the prisoners worked inside the walls making such things as wagons, furniture, shoes, and boots. Others were sent to projects outside the prison, cutting timber, quarrying, or building railroads. In 1872, for example, of the 944 inmates, 306 worked on railroad construction crews, including the Houston and Great Northern.[28]

The industrial contractors who leased the prisoners from Ward, Dewey, and Company were required to guard the prisoners and provide them with the essentials of life. Too often prisoners were beaten, inadequately fed, and forced to sleep in crowded pens. Eventually, public criticism arose, and Governor Richard B. Hubbard terminated the contract with Ward, Dewey, and Company in 1877. Even though the state resumed control of the penitentiary and the convicts, the new strategy did not end the use of the convict lease system, since railroad companies leased the prisoners directly from the state.[29]

Another railroad, chartered on August 5, 1870, was the International Railroad. Its goal was to build from central Texas northeasterly to Arkansas in order to connect Texas with northern rails. Its investors were capitalists from St. Louis and Texas. By that time granting of public lands was not an option, so the legislature supported the endeavor by passing a bond measure that awarded the railroad $10,000 for every mile of track it built. The state comptroller, however, refused to sign the bonds and the state supreme court upheld the comptroller's action. During the political impasse the railroad executives slowly began construction. By the end 1873 the International had laid tracks from Hearne to Palestine and then continued on to Longview giving the company a total of 177 miles of track.[30]

To strengthen both roads, on September 30, 1873, the directors consolidated the Houston and Great Northern with the International and formed the International and Great Northern Railroad. Having constructed direct connections to Houston on the south and Arkansas to the northeast, the railroad executives then laid new plans that included the ultimate goal of extending the railroad westward to the Rio Grande. Within one year of consolidation, 1874, the railroad reached Rockdale, thirty miles from Hearne. All construction material, except the timber products, was shipped through Galveston. There, at Rockdale, the company built a turntable for reversing the engines, and halted further construction for two years as it planned the next phase of construction.[31]

International and Great Northern Railroad route.
Courtesy of David Rumsey Map Collection

During the hiatus from construction the owners of the railroad sold lots in the new town of Rockdale and searched for sources of funding. They also went about securing strips of land two hundred feet wide for the right-of-way westward. One purchase was in the Liendo League from Soledad Liendo of Saltillo, Coahuila. Señora Liendo was the widow of José Justo Liendo who had purchased eleven leagues from the State of Coahuila y Texas in 1828. The strip of land extended for twelve miles west of Rockdale into Williamson County and authorized the free use of earth, material, timber, and rock.[32]

In the meantime the railroad directors and politicians friendly to their cause lobbied the legislature for a law that would require the comptroller to issue the bonds. Opponents of the bond issue, however, warned that the potential debt associated with expanding the railroad through bonds would be huge and equal to all the other expenses of the state government. Land grants regained favor with the politicians and the voters approved of a constitutional amendment that permitted granting public lands, provided that the grants not exceed twenty sections of land for each mile of track.

The I & GN executives actually preferred the bonds, but in 1875 when the politicians proposed granting the new railroad twenty sections of public land for each mile of track laid and no state taxes for twenty-five years, the executives concurred.[33]

The I & GN received 3,339,520 acres of Texas land and in order to turn the acres into dollars, the executives formed a subsidiary, the Texas Land Company. The land company published maps, and advertised the opportunities available in Texas. One brochure proclaimed "Texas Wants one Million Emigrants [sic] for Twenty Years." Palestine served as the administrative center for the efforts and even offered free rooms to land seekers at the Immigrants' Home. In 1879 the Texas Land Company sold its remaining land, 3,049,430 acres to another land company and garnered $4,463,960.[34]

Immigrants Home: The Illusion.
Courtesy David Rumsey Map Collection

Immigrants Home: The Reality.
Source: The Portal to Texas History,
University of North Texas Libraries

Workers resumed construction westward from Rockdale in 1876. The superintendent of construction who directed the project from Rockdale to Austin was Thomas B. Cronin. He had learned the science of laying rails while working for the Missouri Pacific in Sedalia, Missouri, but this was his first Texas project. He promised to lay one mile of track a day, a goal which he met and occasionally surpassed. Convicts also laid the tracks on this section of the road.[35] When the railroad reached Austin in December the I & GN paid Cronin a bonus of $3,000 in cash and awarded him a section of land. Points along the track, such as Thorndale, became transfer places for agricultural goods and grew into towns. After the rails had been laid, Cronin continued working for the railroad and took up residency in Palestine.[36]

In spite of support from the state, the profits were insufficient to bring economic stability. Beginning in 1878 the I & GN went through several reorganizations, mergers, and receiverships until 1925 when it became part of the Missouri Pacific Railroad Company.[37]

The railroads quickly transformed the cattle trade by building directly to the area where the cattle were raised. Although the long drive did not cease immediately, it was just a matter of time, and by the early 1880s the cattle bound for the northern market rode in cattle cars. Thrall, originally called Stiles Siding, five miles west of Thorndale, became the shipping depot for the Olive cattle. And when the railroad continued on another seven miles, Taylor was platted and became an even larger shipping center.[38]

While the railroad boosted the profits of the cattle trade by providing transportation to market, the invention of barbed wire brought an end to the open range. The same year that the railroad reached Rockdale, 1874, Joseph F. Glidden received a patent for inexpensive fencing strong enough to protect crops from cattle. Barbed wire was marketed in Milam County in 1879. Together, the railroad and barbed wire made commercial farming possible, and the grassland of Milam and Williamson could be turned into fields of cotton.

Livestock, corn, and cotton had been the agricultural mainstays before the railroad, but the railroad soon changed subsistence farming to diversified agriculture and eventually to commercial farming. Cotton grew in importance and became the major cash crop. In 1880 Milam County farmers planted 37,473 acres in cotton and in 1900 the number of acres increased to 147,683. The number of bales ginned in 1880 was a mere 10,844 but in 1900 the number was up to 66,555. Corn continued as a significant crop and was largely used for feeding livestock. The increased corn production went from 32,725 acres in 1880 to 71,151 in 1900. Through its extensive marketing capacity, the railroad made it possible to increase the volume of both crops. Seventy-five percent of the improved land was dedicated to just those two crops.[39]

The railroad served the farmer not only by hauling the farm goods away to the market, but it also brought in products for the farmers' use. Wheat flour, for example could be purchased in town at a lower price than the flour would cost if the farmer grew the wheat and had it milled into flour. As a result local wheat production declined significantly. Instead of basing his security on the full smokehouse and cellar as the yeoman farmer did, the new farmer opened an account at the bank and kept an eye on the balance.[40]

The number of residents in Milam County more than doubled between 1870 and 1880, rising from 8,984 to 18,659. Twenty years later, in 1900, the population had more than doubled again and reached a new high of 39,666 residents. Even though the population of towns grew, approximately 75 percent of the residents were rural and the economic life of the towns was dependent on agriculture.[41]

In Williamson cotton production made even greater strides than it had in Milam. Each census reported the growth. Farmers produced 4,217 bales in 1880, 33,945 bales in 1890, and 80,514 in 1900. In 1900 Williamson County ginned more cotton than any county in Texas except Ellis County. Not only did the number of improved acres dramatically expand, so did the proportion of acres planted in cotton. The proportion of crop-land used for cotton production moved from about one-third of the total in 1880 to approximately two-thirds in 1910.[42]

Cotton production, however, was labor intensive. Milam County land owners followed the Southern practice of handling such large acreages in a slave-free society by turning to tenant farming and sharecropping. In 1880 tenants accounted for the operation of nearly a third of the county's 2,219 farms and by the turn of the century they were working 60 percent of the 5,337 farms in the county. In Williamson dramatic changes in land tenure also coincided with the shift to cotton production. As late as 1880, 1,183 of the 1,538 farms, or 77 percent, were still worked by owners. By 1890 only 43 percent of the farms were operated by owners, and the percentage of owner-operators remained at 40 percent until the 1920s.[43]

Racial and Ethnic Composition of Milam and Williamson

Following Emancipation, most of the former slaves in Milam County remained in the county. Some freedmen established little communities such as Liberty Hill or Sneed Chapel and others moved to towns such as Cameron and Rockdale, but the majority was associated with agriculture as farm laborers and sharecroppers. A significant number of blacks owned their own farms. In 1910 blacks owned 1,240 or about 25 percent of the farms in Milam.[44]

The number of black citizens in the county increased steadily, rising from 2,977 in 1870 to a high of 10,473 in 1900. Even as their numbers increased, the proportion of the total population decreased because of the large influx of white immigrants, so that in 1890 they constituted about 25 percent of the population. In 1910 the black population had dropped slightly to 9,487, and comprised approximately 24 percent.[45]

Just as Williamson County's slave population had been less than Milam's so was the black presence in Williamson County less at the turn of the century. Blacks comprised only 17 percent of the population in 1910 and owned less than 1 percent of the farms.

The Census of 1900 listed only five blacks living in the village of Thorndale. During the next ten years that number increased to forty-nine. Most were employed as cooks and servants, porters in hotels and barbershops, and laborers.[46]

Both Milam and Williamson counties witnessed the immigration of Europeans in late nineteenth and early twentieth centuries. The foreign-born population in Milam in 1880 was 499 out of 18,659. And in Williamson County in 1870, only 111 of the residents out of 6,368 were foreign born. Foreign immigration took place after the railroad and barbed wire made settlement of the grassland possible.

These new residents were largely Germans or German-speaking Austrians, but the numbers also included Scandinavians such as the Swedes and Slavic groups represented by the Czechs and the Wends. The proportion of foreign born in both counties remained at about 10 percent or less from 1900 to 1930.

The Wends, one of the ethnic groups that settled in Thorndale and the surrounding land, were part of a little-known Slavic group. The reason for their anonymity is that their number in Europe was small and they never formed their own nation. In Texas they called themselves Wends while in contemporary Europe they identify themselves as Sorbs. At times they are called Serbo-Lusatians because they live in the Lusatian area in the southeastern portion of Germany. Even so, they are Slavic, not Germanic, and their cultural heritage is similar to their Slavic neighbors, the Czechs and Poles.

Their conflict with the Germanic people began in approximately 800 A. D. as the Germanic tribes began moving eastward into the lands occupied by the Wends. During the following centuries the Germans conquered Wendish lands and introduced German rule. By the middle of the nineteenth century, when Wendish migration to Texas began, most Wends lived in the Germanic nation states of Prussia and Saxony.[47]

Even though the Wends became German citizens they suffered from economic discrimination, social segregation, and onslaughts on their culture. The pressure to assimilate into the German culture was strongest in the German-dominated cities and towns. Wends needed to speak German for reasons of employment and even though Wendish families in the early years lived in separate parts of town, association with Germans in the marketplace weakened the Wendish heritage and over time, many became part of the German community.

Other Wends, especially those in the countryside, which is where most Wends who migrated to Texas lived, retained their language and culture. However, even then the German language was inescapable. Young men, for example, learned German as they met their service requirement in the German military. As a result, even in those places that were predominately Wendish, the Wends often became bilingual. Most Wends who migrated to Texas were able to speak German, and all were classified as German citizens.

Because of their knowledge of German they joined the massive German migration in the nineteenth century to many parts of the globe and found new homes in Australia, Canada, South Africa and the United States. En route to their new homes the Wends traveled with Germans and generally joined the German settlements. On occasions their numbers were large enough so they formed Wendish clusters within the German settlements and preserved their language and customs for a while longer.

Besides citizenship and language another unifying aspect between the Germans and Wends was religion. Most of the Wends who migrated were Lutheran and in the new lands, they were willing to accept a German church service if a Wendish one was not available. So the German culture which the Wends resisted in Europe became a comfortable setting for the Wends of Texas. Instead of remaining a Wendish minority as in Germany, the Wends became part of the German minority in Texas and often added English as a third language.

Of all the Wendish settlements outside of Europe, the largest was in Texas, and it was in Texas where the Wendish language and traditions survived the longest. In 1854 the *Ben Nevis* arrived at Galveston with more than 500 Wends who then moved inland into what is now Lee County and formed a Wendish settlement named Serbin. Included in the group was a Wendish-speaking pastor, Jan (Johann) Kilian, who conducted Wendish church services and taught the language to the school children. In the subsequent years and continuing on into the twentieth century smaller groups of European Wends migrated to invigorate the Serbin community and to settle in other parts of Texas. Thorndale was one of these communities where the Wends settled and joined with some Germans to establish a German-speaking Lutheran church.

The Wends are not only an important part of Thorndale's history, but they figure into the lynching of Antonio Gomez. Charles Zieschang, the man slain by Gomez, was of Wendish stock and so was his wife, Anna Moerbe. Four men were charged with the lynching of Gomez and two were part of the Wendish community. There is some irony in the fact that the newspapers in their accounts of the lynching identified them as Germans when in actual fact they had experienced the hardship of minority existence under the European Germans. In fact, their history was parallel to that of the Mexicans born in pre-revolutionary Texas. Both groups became citizens of a foreign nation through conquest and not through a choice of their own. However, the parallel between the Wends and the Mexicans in Texas ended there. The Wends entered the Anglo-Texas world as Germans and within a generation they yet again had assimilated into another linguistic and cultural tradition.

Charles Zieschang's ancestors were the first of the Wends to settle near to what later would become Thorndale. In 1871 Peter Zieschang, the patriarch, purchased land in Williamson County about nine miles from Thorndale. Peter had been born in Kreckwitz, Saxony in 1827, and 1855 he, with his wife and her adopted niece, Magdalena Poldrack, migrated to Australia. Some Wends, including Mrs. Zieschang's relatives, had migrated a few years earlier and formed a small Wendish community in Victoria. The settlement initially was named Hochkirch after a town in Saxony, but later during World War I, when Australians were purging the map from anything German, the name was changed to Tarrington. Two sons were born there, Johann in 1857 and Carl in 1863. In 1859 Zieschang was naturalized as an Australian citizen. For reasons of health he reconsidered his choice of Australia and returned to Europe with his family.[48]

The Australian experience, however, had broadened his horizons and Germany no longer suited him. After a few years he and a number of relatives and friends decided to migrate to Texas. The group of approximately twenty-five Wends traveled to Bremen and boarded the *Frankfort* for New Orleans, arriving on November 15, 1870. From there they traveled by train to Brenham and then by oxcart to Serbin.

After a short stay in Serbin, Peter settled briefly in Travis County near present-day Pfluegerville and then on September 22, 1871, crossed into southern Williamson County and purchased 440 acres for $2,400 along Brushy Creek in the Hamilton White League.[49]

In contrast to the tidy rectangular survey system employed in the northern United States and in north and west Texas, with its base lines and meridians, the system utilized in Williamson County combined aspects of the Spanish method of surveying land with the southern United States system called metes-and-bounds. Distances were measured in varas, compass bearings provided directions, and physical features became points of reference. The boundaries of Zieschang's property, for example included "a China tree 10 inches in diameter" and "a stake for the NW corner on the prairie." However, stakes could be moved and Chinaberry trees could be cut down. Land owners learned the necessity of safeguarding property lines.[50]

The location Zieschang selected was three miles south of the present town of Thrall, and through the years that location went by several names. One was Brushy Creek, named after the creek that flowed eastward and about one mile south of Thorndale. Peter preferred the name Hochkirch, the name used in Australia and Germany, but later it was changed to Noack in honor of the postmaster, Ernst Noack, another Wend. Noack remained a small community because it was bypassed by the railroad and suffered from competition from neighboring Taylor and Thorndale.

Four hundred forty acres was more than he could cultivate, so Zieschang also raised cattle and in 1873 he registered his PZ brand in the Williamson County Brand Book. His holdings were not far from the Olive family properties and there on the frontier of central Texas he entered the arena of the open range, rustling, and guns. The land

Zieschang purchased also straddled the cattle trail used by the Olives to drive the cattle north from their land to the pens near the railroad. The biographer of Print Olive, Harry E. Chrisman, identified Zieschang as "a round headed young German," and reported that the neighbors clashed over the use of the trail.[51]

Peter Zieschang, the immigrant from Central Europe, quickly learned both the importance of protecting property and the workings of the Texas court system. In May 1880 he was fined $200 for breaking down a fence and in January 1881 John and Charles Zieschang pleaded guilty for doing the same thing, but they were fined only $10 and court costs[52]

Members of the extended Zieschang family along with other Wends and German who settled in the Hochkirch area eventually joined to create a congregation. Prior to founding their own church the Zieschangs traveled the fifty miles to Serbin for sacraments of baptism and the Lord's Supper or for worship services. Peter's oldest son, John, born in Australia and veteran of travel across the oceans, was one of the settlers. He had married Maria Theresia Jannasch and in 1879 their first child was baptized by Pastor Kilian in Serbin. Eventually there were eight more children. One of these was Karl, born in 1885, who was the victim of the 1911 stabbing.[53]

The next step in the migration of Wends to Thorndale was made by two brothers, Andreas and Carl August (C. A.) Polnick. Their parents had migrated to Texas in 1853 and after settling first at Rabbs Creek, they eventually settled on the West Yegua in a community later named Fedor. In January 1880 Andreas moved from West Yegua to eastern Williamson County, not far from Noack, and purchased 140 acres of land. C. A. had opened a store at West Yegua in 1877 but in 1882 he sold that store to Fedor Soder and opened a new store in Thorndale. The move may have saved his life because in the next year robbers murdered two men whom Soder had hired to manage his store.[54]

Shortly thereafter, in 1885, Charles Michalk moved his family to Thorndale. Charles had migrated to Texas in 1859 just before the Civil War, but instead of joining the Confederacy, he crossed the Rio Grande into Mexico and then made his way to the coast where he boarded a ship for New Orleans. He fought for the Union and later collected a military pension. He purchased 700 acres of land near Thorndale and with a partner built the first brick building in town and operated a mercantile store.[55]

Jacob Moerbe moved to Thorndale in 1895 in order to be near seven of his nine children who had settled there. He had migrated to Texas in 1854 on the *Ben Nevis* and en route he lost his first wife to cholera. While living near Serbin he married a second time and eventually purchased land at Fedor. His sons continued the economic success that he had achieved, and were profitably engaged in farming, town development, and merchandizing. Both Jacob Moerbe and Charles Michalk were the grandfathers of Anna Moerbe who was widowed on June 19, 1911[56]

In 1890 the Lutherans from Thorndale and Noack united to form a new congregation, St. Paul, and Charles Michalk donated ten acres north of the road to Taylor for a church, school, and cemetery. The congregation continued to grow and in 1893 called a resident pastor. By 1911 the congregation had increased to 654 souls and included in that number was Charles Zieschang, the victim, and two of the defendants, Gerhard Noack and Harry Wuensche.

Although some of the Wends settled in Thorndale and engaged in commerce, the majority occupied the farm land surrounding the town, especially to the north and west in both Milam and Williamson counties.

The Mexican population was numerically among the smaller national groups in the two counties—similar in size to the Wends. Mexican immigration to central Texas reached a significant level in about 1910, just as the European immigration tapered off. The Mexico-born population in Milam County nearly doubled from 479 in 1900 to 871 in 1910. In Williamson County the numbers were slightly smaller, but the percentage was greater. There were 294 residents born in Mexico in 1900 and 732 in 1910.[57]

Most of the Mexicans in the two counties worked in agriculture, either as individuals or family groups on farms, or as gangs of men chopping wood and clearing or "grubbing" land. The census enumerator identified one group as men engaged in cutting cord wood. One reason for the dramatic increase of the Mexican presence in Milam County was the development of lignite mines near Rockdale. Coal deposits had been identified in Milam County as early as the 1860s, but the first mine was not established until 1890. By the mid-1890s the county had six mining operations, producing a total of twenty railcars of coal per day. At its peak between 1910 and 1920 the mines shipped as many as forty-five to fifty cars each day.[58]

Although supervisors and some miners were Anglo American or Europeans, the mine owners recruited workers from Mexico, and in 1910 approximately 330 people of Mexican birth were living in a location seven or eight miles away from Rockdale that was called *La Recluta*. Wives and children were included in these statistics and while they were more often present among those who worked on farms, they were even present among the men who worked in gangs.

The numbers counted as Mexicans in the aggregate census statistics are only those born in Mexico and not their children born in Texas. Thirteen of the 871 Mexico-born residents of Milam County lived in Thorndale in 1910, but not counted in the Mexican group were sixteen children of Mexican heritage who had been born in Texas.

In 1910 Gabriel Gamez was sixty-one years old and worked as a farm laborer in Caldwell County. He had migrated from Saltillo, Coahuila in 1867, returned to Mexico the next year, and came back to Texas, to Comal County, in 1874. His married his first wife, Tomasa Martinez, also a native of Coahuila, in 1880. All of his children were born in Texas and at least two, including Antonio, were baptized in St. Paul and St. Peter church in New Braunfels. Antonio, the victim of the lynching, was born on September 2, 1896, and baptized a year later. Gabriel's first wife died leaving him with five children, but in 1905, while he was living in Caldwell County, Gabriel married Amelia, twenty years his junior. In November 1910 he moved his family to Williamson County, west of Thorndale, where he and Antonio worked for Albert Moerbe clearing the land of mesquite and scrub in preparation for plowing and planting cotton. The family lived in a building provided by Moerbe[59]

By 1910, in spite of the foreign migration, the native born white population maintained its numerical majority in both Milam and Williamson counties. Sixty-eight percent of the people in Milam and 73 percent of Williamson's population were neither foreign born nor black. That strong majority of the native born white population exercised political power in the two counties and it was this group that provided the officials, peace keeping officers, judges, lawyers, and jurors named in the accounts of the trials.[60]

III. THORNDALE 1878–1911

The railroad between Rockdale and Austin had been completed in 1876 and that year Thorndale began its existence as a lowly station stop. The iron horse at that time could travel extended distances between fuel and water stops, but the railroad builders also knew that their business depended on the four-legged horses with lesser rates of speed. Because farmers generally preferred to travel to town and back home on the same day they needed a location within approximately six miles from home. The last town on the railroad was Rockdale so as the railroad moved westward the next stop would be built approximately twelve miles away in order to accommodate the agrarian customers.

The land on which Thorndale was built was owned by Soledad Liendo, the same person who had sold the right of way to the International & Great Northern. On January 12, 1878, William S. Carothers, a cattle dealer from Austin, bought the entire block of 3,760 acres for $2.00 per acre. Most of the Liendo league was located in Milam County, although a corner extended into Williamson.[61]

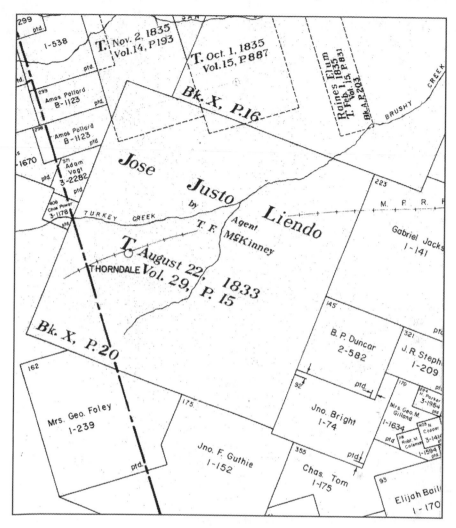

The Liendo Grant.
Courtesy of the Texas General Land Office,
Archives and Records, Austin, Texas

The stop was initially named Everett after Colonel Everett, a railroad employee who was also engaged in marketing real estate. Everett was not located at Thorndale's current location, but it was situated three miles west, in that corner of the Liendo league that lapped over into Williamson

County, near the present city cemetery. Not content with the name Everett, another railroad employee gave it a more descriptive name, Thorndale, because of the numerous mesquite trees and cactus plants in the area. Thorndale's official birthday is April 18, 1878, when the postal service granted the station stop a post office. In addition to the post office and a railroad car that served as the depot, Thorndale was the location for a small store and a hotel.[62]

Possibly it was the steam locomotive's need for water that explains the reason for moving the town eastward. In 1879 the I & GN drilled down 1,800 feet for a well, but the drillers failed to find water.[63] The next year, in 1880, Lewis Carothers bought the store from James K. Quinn and moved the building to Thorndale's present location which today would be the northwest corner of the intersection of Highway 79 and Main Street. There was no guarantee for finding a good well at the new location, but if efforts to strike underground water failed, Brushy Creek could become an alternative source, and it was close enough to Thorndale's new location: less than one mile. The post office's address was officially changed from Williamson to Milam County on June 14, 1880.[64] Other residents followed Carothers eastward, and in the 1880 census his neighbors included a bookkeeper, a stone mason, a carpenter, and a physician, although most of the people in the community were farmers and stock raisers.[65]

An adequate water supply continued to be a major quest at the new location and on March 15, 1881, W. S. Carothers proposed to bore an artesian well on his land near the railroad station. The projected cost would be $6,000 and if the railroad paid one-half of that amount, Carothers agreed to pay the other half and they would share the water. At a time when two dollars bought an acre of land, $6,000 was a formidable amount of money, and whether or not the project went further than the planning stages is not known.[66] Either it was not attempted or they found no water at the new location either, so Brushy Creek became the fall-back site for water. The railroad manager solved the immediate problem and instructed his men to dig a 10 x 10 hole fourteen feet deep near the creek and that surface well then provided suitable amounts of water for the railroad and the town's residents. By 1884 the population reached 130 and in addition to the businesses there was a church and a school. A box car served as the railroad station.[67]

As the steam engines grew in size, so did the capacity to travel longer distances without re-supplying the boiler with water, and smaller water stops such as Thorndale became less important. However, the population of the settlement also grew and so did the need for a water system for people rather than machines. Thorndale's growth in the 1880s and 1890s had been modest, but by 1900 the population was 448 and future growth was dependent on a water supply. In 1902 the editor of the Thorndale newspaper reported that Thorndale had a water works system, but no water. One solution would have been to clean out the old railroad well and dig it deeper while another option was to build a dam and create an artificial lake. Creating such a reservoir was the better alternative, but it was more expensive, and by 1904 there was still no lake.[68]

At the turn of the century Thorndale's merchants continued with the town's initial economic mission of providing goods for the rural customers, but as the population increased, the merchants also catered to the needs of the town's residents. The stores stocked dry goods: men's suits and women's hats as well as work clothes, groceries that ranged from freshly butchered meat to evaporated apples, and general merchandise including washing machines, sewing machines, and Victor record players. The railroad provided direct transportation to St. Louis and Thorndale merchants traveled there to order items that included the most modern equipment and embodied the latest styles. These business trips enabled them to enjoy the big city and in 1904 some citizens of Thorndale sent seventeen car loads of cattle to St. Louis and went along in order to attend the World's Fair.[69]

In addition to the suppliers of merchandise there were also providers of services who in 1900 included three blacksmiths, a maker of saddles and harnesses, and three saloon workers. The medical profession, seemingly over-represented, included three physicians and six druggists. There was only one resident clergyman, a Lutheran, and two teachers. The presence of five carpenters gave evidence of Thorndale's entrance into a period of growth. Thorndale also had a bank, two hotels, two cotton gins, a livery stable, a printing office, and a short-order restaurant. And finally, there was the telegraph operator who symbolized the modern era. His presence was directly associated with the railroad, and the railroad and the telegraph broke the rural isolation and connected Thorndale with the world. Ties with the outside world were not always as simple as it would seem and although Thorndale had "a pretty depot," the editor complained that Thorndale had the "darndest inconvenient train schedule of any town on the road."[70]

Ten years later, by 1910, Thorndale's growth had reached full stride. Thirteen men were engaged in construction and painting, and eight made a living selling lumber. Twenty-seven laborers, the largest category for an occupation, were available for any type of work. Seventeen persons worked with dry goods, six in hardware, and eighteen in grocery stores. Six men worked in the cattle trade, four in cotton.

The number of physicians remained at three, but there was one dentist. Medical specialists, such as podiatrists, traveled to Thorndale from time to time and received their patients in a room at the Commercial Hotel, which advertised a room for $2.00 a night.[71] Other service employees included four workers in a bank, six barbers, two furniture salesmen, one insurance agent, two editors, and a tailor. The number of clergymen increased to four and there were six teachers.

Not all of the residents were part of a family nor did they plan to make Thorndale a permanent home. Many were single people looking for work while others were older people, widows and widowers, who needed temporary shelter. Thirty-five persons of all ages, but primarily young men, boarded with families or found rooms in the three small hotels. Catering to this transient population were four restaurants that employed five people and five saloons employing ten workers.

The female presence may have been less visible, but it was there. In an era when women wore hats there were four milliners, as well as one dressmaker, two confectionery workers, one baker, and one jeweler. Twenty-three women held jobs other than housewife, usually as clerks or cooks. Three of the six teachers were women.

Some occupations hinted of modern times. Two men, symbols of the industrial era, but men whose counterparts were found in towns along the railroad, managed the depot and railroad business. Two other persons identified themselves as mechanics. One was electrical and the other worked with automobiles. The young man who operated the automotive garage was Charles Zieschang who would be killed on June 19, 1911. In December 1909 he had arranged for the construction of a house in Thorndale and then moved from his home eight miles southwest of Thorndale, near Noack, to Thorndale. He had married a local girl and was the father of four young children.

But Thorndale continued to resemble a nineteenth-century village. Transportation was either by railroad or by horse. Five men were blacksmiths, four worked at the livery stable, and eight worked on a dray line, most likely hauling cotton.[72]

In order to transform Thorndale from a nineteenth-century village into a booming, bustling twentieth-century town, Thorndale needed to complete several projects. The first task was to confront the problem of an adequate water supply. That continued to be a vexing issue and because Thorndale was not incorporated, the water system depended on private enterprise. Some entrepreneurs, in the years following 1904, had developed a dammed lake and two men, Andrew J. Urban and A. J. Lehman, constructed a cistern in town atop a tower forty feet high. Its capacity was two hundred barrels of water. Although not every home in town was served by this system, it did provide water for the business section and nearby residences. Unfortunately, in February 1909, at 10:00 in the morning the tower gave way, sending the tank crashing to the ground.[73]

The businessmen met to discuss the dilemma and most of them favored incorporating the town so that a small tax could be levied that would provide revenue for a water system. The individuals who had already invested their money in the lake and pipes, however, were not interested in the proposal unless they had some guarantee for their investment. Finding no simple solution, the businessmen then selected a committee to study the problem. The committee's solution was to continue with Urban and Lehman, so the two financed the construction of a new fifty-one-foot tower made out of steel, not wood, and crowned it with an "iron clad cistern." They also replaced the small pipes on Main Street with a three-inch main and added two fire hydrants and a public watering trough.[74]

A set-back, however, occurred four months later when Mrs. Lehman attempted to start the gasoline engine that operated the water pump used to fill the cistern. The gasoline overflowed and ignited a fire on the engine, which spread and destroyed both the engine and the building. The fire was inopportune in that the steam engines at two of the cotton gins relied on that water system, and the picking season was well underway.[75]

The effect of the misfortune was temporary and no one lost his resolve to find a solution. Further motivation for a solution came from Thorndale and Rockdale businessmen who were making plans to construct a cottonseed oil company for Thorndale. A dependable water supply was a necessity for such an enterprise, so the water company was reorganized and the investors of the oil company bought a large portion of the water company stock. In December the new water company cleaned and enlarged the lake, doubling its capacity and thereby ensuring a supply of water sufficient for the next cotton season.[76] With that venture the problem of an adequate water supply was finally resolved and Thorndale's growth was no longer threatened. In 1911, when electricity became almost as desired as water, Thorndale's businessmen combined the two utilities and on September 21, 1911, incorporated the Thorndale Water and Light Company with $10,000 capital stock.[77]

One of the leading promoters of Thorndale was E. L. Ramsey, editor of Thorndale's newspaper, *The Thorndale Thorn*. From the time it was first organized on October 5, 1900, to the time it became the *Thorndale Champion*, growth was the newspaper's prominent theme. Brick construction presented a greater permanence than construction with wood, and one of Ramsey's first projects was to encourage citizens to build brick houses instead of frame. In issue after issue he happily reported when a brick house was planned, how it was progressing, and when it was occupied. "Thorndale," he stated, "is building faster than any other town in this part of the state."[78]

The Thorndale Thorn office.
Courtesy of Patricia Swayze Larsen

Even more than brick houses, he approvingly reported on the construction of brick buildings in the business district. These buildings were often two stories high, between 30 to 40 feet wide and 80 to 100 feet deep, with a plate glass window, a cement sidewalk, and a verandah. In June 1907 he wrote, "Steadily and surely Thorndale is forging ahead. Who will be next?" [79]

The first brick commercial building had been built in 1902 by John A. Michalk, owner of the Thorndale Mercantile Company. Several more brick buildings followed but 1909 and 1910 were the banner years. In January 1909 Michalk began a second brick building, 30 by 100 feet in size, a "double-decker" with a cement sidewalk. When completed it housed the A. M. Waiser furniture store and the post office. At that time the Newton-Strauss building was nearing completion and so was another brick building owned by John Kieschnick.[80] The most impressive was the First National Bank's new building with construction costs of $10,282. It had a slightly smaller footprint than the other buildings, 30 by 65, but it was two stories high, and was built with brick manufactured in St. Louis. The building and the bank it housed conveyed stability with three large marble columns in front and a stone eagle above the entrance. "To be sure, Thorndale is growing some."[81]

Thorndale Mercantile Company, circa 1909.
Also known as the Michalk Building.
Courtesy of Edward Bernthal

Thorndale Main Street, circa 1914.
The sign on the Michalk building reads: GOOD
ROADS WILL PUT DOLLARS IN YOUR
POCKETS. *Courtesy of Bill E. Biar*

Contemporary view of the Michalk building.

One of the buildings that pleased the editor was the two-story building erected by J. S. Gore and F. J. Smith in 1904. The upper story was occupied by a fraternal lodge, the Woodmen of the World, which offered insurance and sought ways to help improve the community. A small portion was set aside as the lodge room, while the remainder became Thorndale's Opera House, including a stage and seating for 250. The Opera House became a social center and in 1907 hosted a masked ball. In 1909 "Herrman and Renos Own Big Company" presented a program of magic, acrobats, and musical comedy. And that same year T. M. Carr, the jeweler, traveled to Dallas and obtained a "moving picture apparatus" so that he could give two or three shows a week.[82]

If expansion was the goal of the Thorndale town fathers, Thorndale needed to broaden its economy beyond just services and merchandise. The only realistic venture would be one built on cotton. Thorndale was already providing services for the cotton farmers. Once the cotton was picked, the farmers needed cotton gins to separate the seeds from the fibers and compresses to shape the cotton into bales. One of several gins in town,

Urban and Sons, enlarged its gin in 1906 so that it could process seventy bales a day. In April 1909 the Farmers' Gin and Compress Company was created with a capital stock of $25,000. The optimistic editor of the *Thorn* predicted that "Thorndale will have more gins and better gins than any town in the state according to its size."[83] The final step in processing cotton was made by draymen who hauled the bales to the railroad's loading platform for shipment to the textile mills.

Cotton fiber for cloth was the primary objective of cotton production, but two-thirds of the weight of cotton picked in the fields came from seeds and those seeds held the potential for greater financial returns. Previously, seeds had been a nuisance and were discarded, but because of the weight and volume even the disposal of seeds was a significant problem.

After the Civil War businessmen and scientists began searching for commercial uses of cottonseed. The early attempts successfully used the oil in cooking and in making soap but an unpleasant odor prevented it from being used commercially. A breakthrough came in 1899 when David Wesson, a chemist employed by the Southern Oil Company of Philadelphia developed a process for deodorizing cottonseed oil. Cottonseed oil revolutionized the cooking oil industry. Compared to olive oil, it was inexpensive and plentiful, and in comparison to butter and lard, it had a higher smoking point. Best of all, it carried the flavor of the food. In 1911, the year of the Thorndale lynching, Procter & Gamble introduced another food product from cottonseed oil: Crisco. When hydrogen was added to the fatty acid chain, the oil hardened to a consistency resembling lard. P&G promoted its new product claiming that it was cheaper than butter and more healthful than animal fats.

But there was more to be utilized from the seed than cooking oil. Oil was only 15 percent of the seed. Twenty-five percent was the hull, or outside shell, and 45 percent was cake or meal, the compound that had contained the oil. Hulls could be used as roughage for cattle, and the meal or cakes served as a feed supplement for cattle. Ten percent of the seed was linters, the fuzz that adhered to the outside of the hull. It was used for padding in furniture and production of paper. Only 5 percent of the seed was discarded.

Because of the bulky nature of the seed, it was necessary to build small processing plants, or oil mills, near cotton gins. So while the fiber was shipped to distant textile mills in factory towns, cottonseed was hauled to the oil mills scattered throughout the cotton producing area. The first cottonseed mill in Texas had been constructed at Schulenburg in 1867, and by 1911 there were 207 mills in the state.[84] Thorndale with its gins and railroad connection was a perfect location for an oil mill. A group of developers from Rockdale and Thorndale took up the challenge, formed the Cotton Oil Company, and capitalized it for $25,000. Ramsey had boosted an oil mill for Thorndale as early as 1903. Finally, in 1909 he was able to report the existence of the project and predicted that "The mill will be a great benefit to Thorndale." In March 1910, the company purchased two acres of land and began construction. By mid-November the mill began crushing cottonseed and was running day and night.[85] The oil mill became a permanent fixture in Thorndale and continues to operate in Thorndale into the twenty-first century.

The Oil Mill.

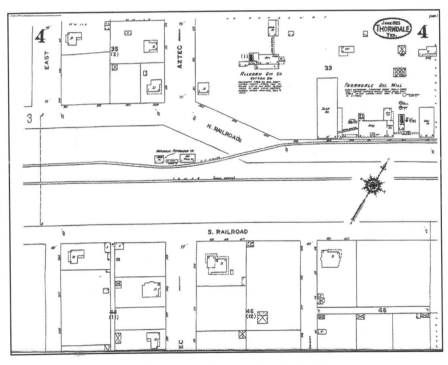

Sanford Map showing the Oil Mill.

Good Roads and the Automobile

The need to build railroads sidetracked the development of local and country roads. While the state provided assistance for railroad construction, local roads were the responsibility of local governments. Not only in Texas, but throughout the United States, merchants, farmers, and even cyclists, realized that existing roads were inadequate and something needed to be done. In Texas the clamor for improved roads coincided with the use of the automobile, but the movement already had been underway in other parts of the United States in the 1890s. Businessmen readily understood that good roads enabled customers to travel to town in wet weather as well as in dry.

Thorndale hosted a meeting for good roads as early as July 10, 1903. There were no tangible results and the fear of increased taxes most likely dulled the fervor for action. The editor of the *Thorn* did not let the matter die and for the next several years the *Thorn* intermittently printed instructions for constructing good roads inexpensively as well as illustrations for improvising road-building equipment. Proponents for improved roads did not insist on expensive macadam roads, but were satisfied with roads made of gravel or sand-clays. Even modest proposals brought little response and by 1910 Milam County reported only twenty miles of improved roads. At the same time Milam County had 107 miles of railroad.[86] For practical transportation and travel, nothing changed, and the railroad and horse-drawn vehicles predominated.

It was the automobile that invigorated the good roads movement in Texas and provided the incentive for moving beyond the gravel roads to paved or macadamized roads. Horse-drawn wagons did not travel appreciably faster on macadam than they did on gravel, but the automobile's speed was variable and macadam reduced the dust and potholes. In 1909 the railroad delivered a carload of asphalt to Thorndale, presumably for macadamizing Main Street. The *Thorn's* editor, in 1910, changed his appeal from simple good roads to macadam roads and proposed funding the paved roads with either a bond issue or a precinct tax. Macadamized roads and the automobile, he predicted, meant more trips to town and from greater distances, and that meant more business.[87]

At least Williamson County citizens listened and in February 1911 the county "let a contract to macadamize ... the public road" (now highway 79) from Taylor eastward to the Milam County line. By May, the crews were macadamizing the road near Thrall, more than half of the way to Thorndale. The Thorndale businessmen finally sprang into action and formed a new association to improve the mile of public road leading from the county line to town.[88]

At the turn of the century any automobile in Texas had been a curiosity. Ten years later, in 1910, they had become status symbols and there were approximately 30,000 cars in the state. Autos were expensive, costing approximately $1,500 each, and the owners were generally bankers, businessmen, or wealthy landowners. Without good roads, the use of cars was restricted, and most were owned by residents in the cities with improved streets. Dallas County led the state with 1,390.[89]

But the future belonged to the car. Even as a status symbol, the car, in certain settings, provided speed and convenience, and it could be practical in hauling people and goods. So the evolution of the car continued. Henry Ford began producing the Model T in 1908 at a affordable price and fuel for the engine was inexpensive. Petroleum, throughout the last half of the nineteenth century was prized as the source of kerosene, an inexpensive substitute for whale oil. Gasoline, another byproduct of petroleum, had been discarded until it became the fuel for the internal combustion engine. Even as the life expectancy of a car increased over time, it required frequent repair. That necessity provided opportunities for men with a knowledge of mechanics to open garages to service the autos. Instead of shoeing horses, men were tinkering with cars. In 1909 Thorndale had its own garage and Charles Zieschang was the owner.[90]

Zieschang in a hot air balloon.
Inscription reads: "bin in Luftschiff 200 feet in
the Luft." His mixing of German and English
words is typical of Germans making the transition
to English. *Courtesy of Roy H. Zieschang*

The first automobile in the neighboring town of Taylor had been acquired by a banker-businessman in 1908.[91] Thorndale was not far behind. The first reference to automobile ownership in Thorndale was on July 23, 1909. The *Thorn* reported that Charles Michalk and Oscar Weiss bought a new black "motor surry" and "they are now trying their patience and learning to operate the machine." The next month five men traveled to Waco and returned with six autos. E. A. Johnson, Zieschang's partner, and Albert Moerbe, who would hire Gabriel Gamez the next year, each purchased a runabout and M. B. Leach obtained a touring car. The remaining three cars carried the Reo brand. Zieschang and Ezra Stephens also made the trip.[92]

Albert Moerbe.
Courtesy of Roy H. Zieschang

Charles Zieschang, Albert Moerbe, and Otto Zieschang.
Courtesy of Roy H. Zieschang

Zieschang and Leach returned to Waco in January and purchased two new model Reo touring cars. The love affair with the automobile was underway and the editor of the *Thorn* wrote "They are four-cylinder shaft drive types and are beauties." In March Zieschang and three men took the train to Dallas where they bought two four-cylinder, twenty-horse Hupmobile runabouts, which "are very pretty make of machines." Zieschang and his partner not only repaired and serviced autos, but also rented them.[93]

The roads and cars made recreational travel possible, and in June nine young men, including Ezra Stephens, Charles Zieschang, and Harry Wuensche, drove to Taylor to see a baseball game between Taylor and Bastrop teams.[94] Zieschang personified the era of the automobile and on Monday June 19, 1911, someone took a photograph of him, tall and husky, dressed in work clothes in front of a brick building. By that night he would be dead.

The earliest owners of autos had been professionals in towns and cities, but with the construction of macadamized roads, the leading purchasers of autos were farmers.[95] The good roads brought more customers to Thorndale, but ironically, also made it possible for people to bypass Thorndale and do business in larger towns such as Taylor and Rockdale. Both were a bare twelve miles away on either side of Thorndale, and the 1909 speed limit of eighteen miles an hour, enabled law-abiding citizens to make the trip in less than an hour. While the railroad provided the justification for Thorndale's existence and growth, the auto would limit its growth and Thorndale was destined to remain a small town. Thorndale's population was 750 in 1910, crested at 1,500 in the late 1920s, and declined to 898 in 1940.

Final Touches of Modernization

Unlike the water supply, two fixtures of the modern age, the telegraph and the telephone, were not projects that required local leadership and broad citizen support. The telegraph came with the railroad and access to it was in the railroad station. The telephone was a service offered by companies that paid for the installation of lines and equipment in the hope of finding enough subscribers for their service. Development began in the cities with dense populations well before lines were strung to the small towns. Even though Austin received its mutual telephone exchange in 1881, Thorndale did nothing about obtaining an exchange until 1909. Once installed, however, the exchange enabled people to acquire phones and greatly simplified the process of phoning others. One year later, at the end of 1910, the Thorndale telephone directory listed nearly three hundred phone customers.[96]

Electrical power, on the other hand, was more like the water system and required local initiative. Transmission of electricity over long distances was not economical so each urban center needed its own generator for producing power for trolley cars, making ice, and lighting homes. By 1890 several Texas cities had their own electric companies. Thorndale became electrified at about the same time it received the telephone, but electrical use was on a much smaller scale.

Zieschang and Johnson, pioneers with the automobile, were also the first to provide electricity. They simply installed a gasoline engine and connected it to a dynamo. The service was available for businesses and residences and was capable of powering sixty to a hundred lights. One of the customers was the Woodmen of the World Opera House. Wilford Wilson, whose primary job was delivering rural mail, also managed the opera house and directed the wiring of the stage and hall with electric lights. Wilson also booked events and the first performance available under electric lights was a traditional vaudeville act that included a moving picture show.[97]

The extent and success of the Zieschang and Johnson enterprise is not known, but at least it showed that electrical service was feasible and soon other entrepreneurs began planning on a larger scale. In October 1910 the Thorndale Light Company promised residents free wiring for their houses if they applied before the end of the month. There must have been setbacks, however, and by the end of the year, E. A. Clark sold the company to E. L Roseberry and E. L. Miertschin who promised "to improve the service." The new owners first provided electricity using the engine at the Miertschin-Elliott gin and then in May of 1911 the Thorndale Light and Power Company installed a new gasoline engine and lit their first lights on May 24, 1911.[98]

With most of the features of a modern town in place, all that remained were some final touches to the beautification of the town and generation of civic pride. One such project was the pouring of cement sidewalks. Businessmen added sidewalks when they constructed their brick buildings, but cement sidewalks were also desirable for the residential area. Contractors from Taylor and Rosebud came to Thorndale in 1911 and offered their services to the citizens. The editor of the *Thorn* listed the persons who accepted the offers and by the middle of March one mile of sidewalks had been poured. And by the end of the month the total was a mile and one-half.[99]

While the annoyance of mud could be resolved with sidewalks, the owners of stray cows were not as easy to deal with. "The cows are becoming a nuisance. Many of them never leave the streets and when a farmer comes to town with a load of corn, he cannot leave the wagon to shop unless he has someone who will protect the load…. It is nothing unusual for one of these old cows to drag a sack of flour, meal or bran from the wagon, tear it and strew its contents on the street." Possibly some owners cooperated and penned their animals, but the next year one cow, named "Old Pide" continued to wander the streets. The editor, equally as relentless, sustained his crusade for beautification and animal control and wrote: "let's put down walks, set out trees, and pen 'Old Pide.'" [100]

The city fathers, on several occasions, brought in business and showed off the town through barbeque picnics and Old Settlers Reunions. One, held in May 1904, attracted 4,000 to 5,000 people. The next picnic in June 1906 was not as successful and attendance was dampened by rain.[101] Four years later, in 1910, another event was scheduled for June. Governor T. M. Campbell agreed to give the opening speech and more speeches followed by fraternal leaders and more politicians. There was also a baseball game (Fats vs. Leans), sack races, a merry-go-round, side shows, and music by the Brenham 2nd Regimental Band. The railroad enticed travelers with special excursion rates, and the measure of success was not in the number of people who attended but in the consumption of barbeque: thirty-five beeves. So optimistic was the editor that he even began talking about purchasing land and constructing an exhibition hall in order that Thorndale could host a fair. Such an event would attract investors and possibly a cotton mill.[102]

Thorndale was prospering and an executive of the I & GN, named T. C. Rodey, toured Thorndale's stores in May 1911 and was impressed by the amount of stock the stores carried. He considered Thorndale, from the commercial standpoint, to be "one of the best towns in this division of his road." Farmers around Thorndale had produced 9,666 bales during the 1909 to 1910 season. Rodey planned to enlarge the cotton platform and make other improvements to the facilities.[103]

Not only did Thorndale use the railroad for bringing in commodities and sending out cotton, it also shipped out other agricultural goods. Examples include a carload of 1,400 turkeys valued at $1,000.00; four carloads of hogs, 269 head, shipped to Houston; and five carloads of potatoes for Chicago and St. Louis.[104]

Thorndale was not an isolated, backward town with a benighted citizenry. Instead it was a modern community dedicated to progress and radiating optimism. From that perspective an act of lynching would be considered an anachronism and unimaginable. Ironically it was civic pride and the fight against litter that set the stage for tragedy.[105]

Social Diversity

Although the *Thorndale Thorn* is silent on social divisions in the town, Thorndale was not the homogenous town often portrayed in descriptions of a Southern lynching. Thorndale, without doubt, was a white man's town but there were small cracks in the social foundation. One group, generally native born of Southern origins, affiliated with Calvinist churches such as the Methodist and Baptist, and adopted a political position that supported prohibition. The Calvinist fervor for prohibition, however, was not sufficiently strong to conquer loyalty to the Democratic Party, and in the gubernatorial election of 1911 only twenty-nine people in all of Milam County voted for the Prohibition Party candidate. One thousand eight hundred and ninety-eight voted for the Democrat candidate, Oscar Colquitt, who opposed prohibition.[106]

This Anglo group included the most socially active residents and their doings were generally reported in the *Thorn*. Comprising approximately 60 percent of the population of Thorndale, these Southern whites were almost exclusively the officials and political leaders. They also controlled the public school system and most of the teachers and students were from this group. And finally, this group provided the membership pool for the fraternal lodges such as the Masons, the Odd Fellows, and the Woodmen of the World.

The smaller portion of the population constituted about 38 percent of the population and was composed largely of immigrant Germans and Wends, or their native-born descendants, who also spoke German. They were Lutheran and stood firm in their opposition to prohibition. Most of this group also voted for the Democratic Party, although the few Republicans in the community originated from this group. For example, the postmaster Gerhard Dube was appointed by a Republican president and Charles Michalk as a veteran of the Union Army received a pension for military service. St. Paul congregation also maintained a parochial school which included instruction in German.[107]While the Calvinist faithful were united in their support of fraternal lodges, there was a difference of opinion among the German Lutherans. The Missouri Synod congregation, St. Paul, prohibited its members from joining lodges largely because of the religious component in lodge rituals. On the other hand, St. John, located in Detmold, a few miles north of Thorndale, and a member of the Texas Synod, did not object to its members affiliating with lodges.

A reliable indicator of the social division was the choice of marriage partner. People generally chose their partners from their religious and ethnic group, and the newspaper announcements of the *Thorn* documented the choices. Such decisions made sense especially for the Lutherans because the use of German in church services would complicate a marriage for one who spoke only English.[108]

In spite of these subtle divisions in Thorndale, there was a visible toleration of the differences. And the lines of separation were not impenetrable. There was some social exchange between groups at picnics and entertainment events, some intermarriage, and an occasional business partnership between members of the two groups. Even if there had been any discord, it most likely would not have been reported in the pages of the *Thorn*. Business was the unifying factor. Businessmen catered to everyone. Symbolic of this attitude was the practice demonstrated by an Anglo-owned store Smith-Bunting, when it advertised its wares in both English and German.

Smith-Bunting advertisement in *Thorndale Thorn*.
The advertisement notified the thrifty
Germans of reduced prices for goods that were
overstocked, slightly damaged, or outdated.

IV. THORNDALE'S
LEGACY OF VIOLENCE

General Conditions after the Civil War

The Civil War laid the groundwork for a perfect storm of violence in Texas. Everything from the blood-letting associated with the war itself, to the dissolution of the system of law enforcement, to the new social setting which included the freed slaves—all coincided to set the stage. As early as April 1865 when word of Lee's surrender reached Texas, most units melted away and the men returned to their homes. But presaging future violence some demoralized Confederate troops, not willing to return empty-handed, looted military stores and stables and sacked towns such as Hempstead. Federal troops arrived in June, but their numbers were too small to simultaneously protect the borders of Texas and to ensure tranquility in the settled areas.

Conditions conducive to law and order remained elusive while the political leaders attempted to draft a new constitution and lay the foundation for a civilian government. Old grudges and conflicting philosophies emerged while Democrats opposed the newly empowered Republicans, and the Republicans quarreled among themselves. However, under congressionally mandated Reconstruction, each rebellious state was required to write a new constitution and Texas complied by assembling a convention on June 1, 1868. The Committee on Lawlessness and Violence, which studied law enforcement, reported that from the end of the Civil War to the summer of 1868, thirty-seven months, 509 whites and 468 blacks had been murdered.[109]

Following ratification of the new constitution and during the statewide elections held in 1869, racial politics added another dimension to Texas violence. Democrats, seeking a return to office, terrorized the freedmen in order to prevent them from supporting the Republicans. In Milam County, for example, as an army officer was escorting approximately one hundred freedmen to the polls in Cameron, a mob of white men attacked the polling place and closed it down before the blacks could vote.[110] But Democrats also intimidated white Republicans. Threats and intimidation discouraged citizens from holding public office under the Republican administration and from 1865 to 1869 more than a third of county offices in Milam County were vacant. One resident wrote "Union men are very scarce in the county, and are afraid to accept office under the present administration."[111]

The newly elected Republican governor, Edmund J. Davis, became the provisional governor on January 8, 1870, and was formally inaugurated as governor on April 28, 1870, thereby ending military rule in Texas. Two major issues facing Davis were the development of the state's economy and establishing law and order. Law and order was needed not only for the general welfare but also specifically for the protection of the freedmen who constituted a cornerstone for his party's survival. The Republican legislature responded by authorizing a militia, which in addition to protecting the frontier, would obey the governor's orders in the event of a declaration of martial law.

A second agency to ensure domestic tranquility was a state police force that was empowered to assist local law enforcement officers. The Police Act of 1870 called for a force of 257 men, including freedmen, with authority to arrest offenders if "local law officers failed to do so." The force never staffed more than 200 persons and some men in that number were unfit to serve. Even so, in 1871 they made 3,602 arrests and in 1872 there were 1,204 arrests. Governor Davis controlled the force, thereby enabling the opposing Democrats to charge him with employing unwarranted executive power to entrench his party in state offices. In 1872, when the Democrats gained control of the lower house of the legislature, they disbanded the state police force and limited the power of the state militia. And the following year, 1873, the Democrats defeated Davis and began their one-hundred-year-domination of Texas government.[112]

The Texas Rangers

The same Democrats who terminated the state police, also voted to scrap the Reconstruction Constitution, and by 1876 a new constitution, more to their liking, was ratified. In reaction to the perceived abuse of power by the chief executive, the new constitution placed greater restraints on the power of state officials. The new constitution further mandated that the office of constable would be the foundation for maintaining law and order and that a constable would be elected for each precinct in the county.[113] Incorporated towns could elect a marshal, and the county sheriff, also elected, was responsible for the entire county and would support the marshals and constables. Thorndale was not incorporated until 1923 and therefore the law in Thorndale was enforced by a precinct constable and the county sheriff.

Even before the new constitution was ratified, Democrat Governor Richard Coke and the legislature, aware of the need to supplement the power of local authorities, revived a paramilitary group: the Texas Rangers. That name had been around a long time, but there was no institutional continuity between the various groups that served under the Ranger name. Not only did the names of the groups vary, but so did the objectives, and there were periods in Texas history when there were no Rangers at all.

Historians trace the Rangers' origins in Texas to 1823, two years after empresario Stephen F. Austin initiated Anglo American colonization in Texas. As the empresario, Austin was responsible for the colony's defense and he hired ten experienced frontiersmen as "rangers" to launch a punitive action against a band of marauding Indians. Not until November 24, 1835, in the opening days of the Texas Revolution, was the group institutionalized by Texas lawmakers as a specific force.

Victory at San Jacinto may have gained independence, but independence did not translate into prosperity. Throughout the ten years of the Republic's existence, the government labored under economic stringency and it was unable to underwrite a military force large enough to suitably defend its citizens against Indian attacks or military incursions from Mexico. At best the Congress fell back on earlier solutions and created a system of volunteer units along with a ranging company. In keeping with previous practice the Rangers wore no uniforms or badges and provided their own weapons and horses—all for a dollar a day of service. The most celebrated incident involving the Republic's Rangers was in 1844 when the unit led by John

"Jack" Coffee Hays first employed the Colt revolvers in a battle with the Comanche Indians.[114]

Following the annexation of Texas in 1846, the United States assumed responsibility for frontier and border protection, so the Ranger force also became a volunteer force that could be called up only if the need arose. Following the Civil War, for a period of several years, there was no Ranger force at all.

When the Republican legislature created the State Police in 1870 it also authorized Davis to raise twenty companies of Rangers for the western and southern frontiers. Inadequate funding terminated the Rangers after less than a year and the legislature returned to the more frugal minuteman concept. Neither approach, ranging companies or minutemen, was effective at controlling such a vast area. In their search for effective law enforcement, however, the Davis legislature initiated two innovations that later became practice. The first was the stipulation that the State Police force was given the entire state as its area of jurisdiction and the second required all three groups, the Rangers, the militia, and the State Police to report to the Adjutant General, part of the executive office.[115] Even though the Democrats ended the State Police force after two years, the Republican structure became a model for the new Ranger force that the Democrats later established.[116]

The Democrats' legislation in 1874 that revived the Rangers not only incorporated both policies, statewide jurisdiction and executive control of the agency, but it also broke with the early Ranger tradition of the citizen-soldier who enlisted for a few months as the need arose, and instead created a permanent force composed of men who served for more than a year. For the first time the Rangers became police officers. Statewide authority, envisioned to increase the effectiveness of the Rangers, however, created conditions for potential tension over jurisdiction between the local law enforcement and the Rangers. Even though the Rangers could make an arrest, the subsequent aspects of the justice process remained in local control and arrests did not guarantee conviction. In keeping with the earlier Ranger groups, the new Rangers, officially called the Frontier Battalion, continued the informal relationships between officers and men, and the manner of dress.[117]

The Indian raids into Texas were soon terminated by United States military forces under the command of General Philip H. Sheridan, thereby enabling the Rangers to focus on the Mexican border and statewide law enforcement. Demands on Ranger intervention fluctuated on these two remaining assignments, but it was Ranger activity along the Rio Grande that provided the most examples of Ranger excesses, which in turn engendered hostility among the Mexican residents.

A popular example of the Rangers' work against lawbreakers within the state was the killing of Sam Bass at Round Rock, a town in Williamson County and less than thirty miles from Thorndale. The killing of Sam Bass was within the law, but it was instant justice through violence. Robert Utley, in his study of the Texas Rangers, places the Rangers into a "six-shooter culture." It was a culture in which the lawmen did not hesitate to shoot, and if conditions did not warrant shooting, physical violence such as a pistol barrel to the head was an option. Physical force was part of law enforcement.[118]

In 1878, two years after the railroad created Thorndale, the Rangers confronted Sam Bass's gang at Round Rock. Bass had begun his outlaw career in 1877 robbing stagecoaches and trains. So notorious were his exploits that the Adjutant General of Texas assigned a company of Rangers to apprehend Bass and his gang. The outlaws eluded the Rangers until July 19, 1878, when the gang rode into Round Rock intending to rob the bank. A member of the gang had turned informant, however, and the Rangers were prepared to apprehend the outlaws. A gun battle ensued in which Bass was mortally wounded. He managed to get on his horse and rode three miles out of town to an oak thicket, and when the Rangers found him, they knew Bass was near death. He died of his wounds on July 21, 1878.[119]

After two decades of successful law enforcement and the emergence of a more stable Texas society, the Rangers became superfluous and the Ranger Frontier Battalion was abolished in 1901. Its replacement, the Texas State Rangers, was limited to law enforcement and the legislature reduced the force to four companies with no more than twenty men in each company. The Ranger unit was therefore a state police force that performed the same function as local law enforcement, but with statewide jurisdiction. The Texas State Rangers were especially active in the boom towns spawned by petroleum strikes and along the border with Mexico where the Mexican Revolution beginning in 1910 further threatened the stability of the area.[120]

Judging by the number of historical studies of the Rangers, one could conclude that the topic is a popular one. Popular it is, but it is also controversial. Some writers have lauded the work of the Rangers and often romanticized their history. One of these early widely read studies is Walter P. Webb's *The Texas Rangers*. In it Webb focuses on the dramatic exploits of the group and the bravery of certain individuals. On the other hand, there are studies that find the Rangers to be the antitheses of law and order and document their conclusion with examples from Ranger service along the Mexican border. *Gunpowder Justice: A Reassessment of the Texas Rangers* is an example. A valuable study of the Rangers, which is more balanced, is the two-volume work of Robert M. Utley. It was written after the two opposing interpretations had been articulated thereby enabling him to addresses some of the conflicting arguments.[121]

Even though a summary of Ranger history may seem tangential to the study of Thorndale, there are three reasons why it is needed. The initial reason is that the apprehension of Sam Bass illustrates a type of on-the-spot justice that took place in Thorndale's neighborhood and was part of Thorndale's heritage of violence. Another reason is that Rangers actually took part in the investigation of the Thorndale lynching. One Ranger accompanied the Assistant Attorney General to Milam County and another was sent to calm a nervous witness. And finally, the background of the Rangers is given to help explain how the Mexican response to the Thorndale lynching was tied to the Mexican image of the Texas Ranger.

Lynching

Lynching is a term whose meaning varies according to time and place. A working definition, however, would include three elements: 1) an alleged crime or undesired act, 2) a self-appointed response group of more than two people, and 3) the infliction of physical harm, including mortal injury, on a person without granting that person due process of law. Other requisites could be added, and in 1940 the National Association for the Advancement of Colored People included a clause in its definition specifying that the offending group justified its crime "under the pretext of service to justice, race, or tradition." The strict definition of lynching used here does not describe the nature of the violence and is not synonymous with hanging[122]

Scholars trace the origins of lynching back to Virginia during the American Revolution. There, a justice of the peace, Charles Lynch, used more than his allotted authority to intimidate Tories, sympathizers of the British. The practice continued in a minor way until after the Civil War when it expanded to all sections of the country, especially in the South. Lynching appealed to Southerners because of its similarity to the Southern code of honor that demanded that a man respond to personal wrongs; and at the same time it provided a mechanism for controlling society disrupted by the end of slavery.

But the concept of self-redress was not a monopoly of the South. Settlers in the West also subscribed to it and in the days before lawmen were present to protect citizens, it could be a matter of survival.[123] Lynching became engrained in Southern and Western culture and seldom did police officers apprehend members of the lynch mob. Community approval or disapproval of the taking of a life, according to James McGovern, created the theoretical difference between lynching and murder.[124]

As a result of collecting and examining hundreds of lynching incidents and cataloging the details, some broad regional differences of the lynching procedure become apparent. In the South the response group was called the lynch mob, the victims were generally Negroes, death resulted from hanging or burnings, and the body was often mutilated. The members of the mob made no attempt at hiding their identity and the event often took on a festive atmosphere.

In the West the group was called the vigilantes. The victims were primarily whites, death was generally the result of hanging or bullets, there was often a plan of action, including the pretense of a court process, and the vigilantes were known only to each other. The procedures present in these two categories, Western vigilante lynching and Southern mob lynching, are not clear-cut or mutually exclusive: however, they provide a reference point for study.

The two categories are even appraised differently. Theodore Roosevelt, for example, reluctantly acknowledged that Western vigilante lynching "had a most healthy effect," but he condemned Southern mob lynching as a form of anarchy.[125] The apparent resolution for Roosevelt's contradictory positions was that Western lynching, or vigilantism, was justified because it took place in the absence of adequate law enforcement, while Southern lynching occurred in a setting when the mechanisms of law enforcement were in place.[126]

Thorndale's lynching does not specifically fit into either category. There were no Southern features such as sadism, mutilation of the body, and a public spectacle, but neither were there Western aspects such as preliminary planning or a mock trial. Yet Thorndale's lynching met all three requisites in the working definition stated above and contained elements found both in the West and the South. That blending of the two patterns is in keeping with Thorndale's heritage. Williamson and Lee counties gave Thorndale its Western heritage and Milam provided the Southern.

Williamson County, the venue for the Ranger's legitimate use of violence against the Sam Bass gang, was also a hotbed of murder that led to vigilante justice. Two years before Sam Bass was eliminated in Round Rock in 1878, twenty-one men were killed in Williamson County. That lawlessness was largely related to rustling, although deaths from long-term family feuds and drunken brawls at the various saloons helped to raise the total number of fatalities. While the Texas Rangers could target a specific individual or gang with success, maintaining every-day law and order throughout the state was beyond the ability of such a small force.[127]

Even though small fortunes could be made in the cattle industry after the Civil War, it could also be a hazardous business. In the days of the open range, before the barbed wire fence, enterprising men started their herds, or expanded them, by roping unbranded cattle and burning the animals with their brand. A corollary to this legal process was to brand calves, if the mother carried a brand, with the same brand as the mother cow. Although the concept behind branding seems clear-cut, disputes over ownership of cattle were common and often produced violence. Violence also resulted from clearly illegal acts such as killing an animal with someone else's brand and removing the hide for sale. Law enforcement by either state of local agencies was inadequate in such a vast area and incapable of resolving disputes or protecting the ranchers' cattle. The cattleman needed to assume responsibility for protecting his own property.

The Olive family had been engaged in the cattle business since before Williamson County became a county. They utilized the standard method of building a herd by branding wild cattle. But as their herds grew in size, so did the problem of protecting their herds from rustlers who were also trying to build their own herds or were skinning branded cattle for their hides. The rustlers found a haven just to the south of the Olive lands, in neighboring Lee and Bastrop counties, along the Yegua Creek, in a wooded area known as the Knobbs, named after some small hills.[128]

In 1875 the Olives placed a notice on the sheriff's bulletin board in Georgetown warning that "anyone caught riding an Olive horse or driving an Olive cow will be shot on sight." Shortly thereafter, on March 22, 1876, the bodies of two suspected rustlers, Turk Turner and James H. Crow, were found stitched in green cow hides bearing the Olive brand. The men had been killed by the "death of the skins," an old Spanish method of torture. Wrapped alive in fresh or green cowhides, the men were left to die as the sun slowly caused the skins to contract. Because the skins carried the Olive brand, the assumption was that the Olives caught the two men skinning their cattle and murdered them. In the trial that followed, the jurors acquitted the Olives, although many people continued to believe the brothers were guilty. In the next months the bodies of about twelve more suspected thieves were found within a radius of twenty-five miles of the Olive ranch. And on May 22, 1876, two men were found hanging near the Williamson County line.[129]

The surviving rustlers of the Knobbs and Yegua gangs decided to respond with their guns and on the night of August 1, 1876, they attacked the Olive men sleeping in a cabin near the cattle pens. Jay Olive was killed, but the others survived the attack and drove the rustlers away. In retaliation, Print Olive then killed Fred Smith, and Print's brother, Bob, shot Cal Nutt. Both victims were suspected of being the leaders of the gangs. On September 22, 1876, the Olives once more went to Georgetown where the grand jury indicted Print for murder. On October 4, the jury again acquitted him.[130]

The Olives also had problems with neighbors who were not rustlers and interested more in farming than in ranching. Peter Zieschang, who had settled there in 1871, claimed that a cattle trail the Olives used was on his property. Bob Olive and Zieschang frequently exchanged bullets when Bob used the trail, and on September 24, 1876, two days after Print was indicted for murder, Bob and another cowboy beat up Zieschang and his friend Ernest Poldrack. That assault cost Bob $300.[131] At least the Wends were not numbered with the twenty-one murder victims, but Texas law and order may have come as somewhat of a culture shock to the new immigrants.

Although patriarch James Olive would not leave his home in Texas, his sons had had enough; they brushed off the Texas dust from their boots and in 1877 took their herd to Custer County, Nebraska. Their absence, however, did not bring peace to the countryside and violence continued. If there was a moral that could be drawn from the Olive story it would be that a law did not enforce itself and if the established authorities were not available when they were needed, then each man had to defend his rights and property—with violence, if necessary.

A refinement of the Olive approach toward the creation of a lawful society was lynch law enforced by vigilantes. Vigilantism is generally associated with men who had a stake in society, such as property owners, businessmen, miners, and cattlemen, and in a society that needed protection of life and property. Using lawlessness to create lawfulness may seem a bit incongruous, but there were its defenders. Theodore Roosevelt, as previously mentioned, did, and so did Hubert Howe Bancroft, in his two-volume study of California titled *Popular Tribunals.*[132]

Richard Maxwell Brown, a foremost scholar of vigilantism, explains, although he does not justify, the positive aspects of this form of justice and the reason vigilantism was so widespread. Pioneers moved westward faster than the institutions that fostered stability and order. Rather than becoming victims of outlaws or disruptive individuals, the law-abiding citizens used these extralegal methods until traditional institutions could be founded and the established the values of the settled areas confirmed.[133] Carrigan and Webb criticized Brown because his explanation legitimated the actions of the lawbreakers. "There is an implicit presumption in the civic virtue of the vigilantes and the criminal guilt of their victims."[134]

Very often the vigilantes employed extralegal procedures that mimicked the legal system such as an impromptu trial, specific charges, a defense, and a jury. Planning the confrontation could be lengthy and the procedures carried an air of legality, but the execution of the verdict was swift. The punishment varied and included beating, ostracism, intimidation, as well as death. The enforcers disregarded individual rights and the immediate implementation of the death sentence prevented appeal. The victims were generally white, Mexican, or Chinese.

In Texas the central part of the state was a hotbed for vigilante activity and for the period from 1865 to 1900, Brown identified twenty-seven separate occurrences.[135] One of these incidents of vigilante activity is significant because it took place in Thorndale's neighborhood in Lee, Bastrop, and Williamson counties and some of the citizens of Thorndale had ties to the victims.

On November 23, 1883, a double murder took place in Fedor, a small Wendish community in Lee County about thirty-five miles south of Thorndale. Wends began settling along the West Yegua in the 1850s and later, when the land around Thorndale was opened for settlement, many of the next generation moved north. One of these Wends, August Polnick, who owned a little store, was one of the first to move to Thorndale. In 1882 he sold his store to Fedor Soder, a German Jewish immigrant. Soder persuaded the postal authorities to open a post office in his store and the address for the community became Fedor.

Instead of operating the store himself, Soder hired two men to do it. Twenty-nine-year-old Carl O. Keuffel, a former resident of Galveston, was responsible for the store. His clerk, Erwin Wilhelm Mros, was twenty-three years old and a Wend who had migrated in 1882. At about 8:15 just prior to closing time, two robbers entered the store and demanded the money. Keuffel complied with the robbers' demands and handed over the money, an unknown amount, but estimated to be somewhere between $15 and $73. The robbers, however, shot Keuffel in the face at such a close range as to leave powder burns, and then shot Mros in the heart. An early report stated that a boy named Schneider had been in the store, but that he was able to escape through the back door. The next morning a posse found some tracks leading toward Lexington, but no one was captured.[136]

Tracking down the criminals was a monumental task. The area nearby was The Knobbs, home to the persons who had been burrs under the saddle of the Olive operation. With its hills and dense woods the area was a sanctuary for anyone hiding from the law. The inhabitants were well-armed and the rumor had it that when they killed anyone they filed a notch on the handle of the pistol. The outlaws were called "Notch-cutters."

The violence at Fedor soon begat more violence. While the investigation of the Fedor murders continued in the attempt to apprehend the criminals, Deputy Sheriff, Isaac "Bose" Heffington was also shot to death. It was dark and no one witnessed the crime. Jeff Fitzpatrick was the prime suspect but he escaped from the area, supposedly assisted by Haywood Beatty.

Partially in response to the Heffington assassination and partially to curtail the lawlessness associated with the Notch-cutters, the leading citizens of McDade, nine miles away from Fedor, organized themselves into a vigilance committee. To reduce crime they became murderers themselves and on Christmas Eve forty-some masked men went to the Rock Saloon, collected three men, one of whom was accused of stealing horses, and took them out of town and hanged them. The three victims were Thad McLemore, Wright McLemore, and Henry Pfeiffer.

Although the vigilantes hid their identities, six relatives of the three victims suspected the businessmen and rode into McDade on Christmas morning. In later testimony one of the six claimed he had come to town to purchase cartridges so he could shoot some hogs, and another stated he came to town to exchange some boots and buy medicine for a ailing child. Most people, however, believed that the purpose was to intimidate or kill two of the prominent businessmen. Threats and cursing led to a gunfight in which more than sixty shots were fired and after which three men lay dead: two of the relatives and one citizen who was running to assist the businessmen.[137]

The next day, Governor John Ireland called out two units of the state militia, the Brenham Grays and the Hempstead's Johnson Guards. Both units assembled quickly and boarded trains for McDade. Other than bodies laid out in the market house, nothing in the community was unusual, and the peace-keepers returned home.[138]

The only person arrested for the Fedor murders was William Mundine. Earlier, in 1874 he had been found guilty for unlawfully carrying a pistol and was fined $25, and some sources claim that he and not Fitzpatrick murdered Heffington. Mundine's trial for robbery and the murder of Keuffel was held in Giddings on March 22, 1884. Much to the chagrin of the general population Mundine was found not guilty. One observer believed that the prosecution's evidence had been irrefutable, but that the judge's instructions made conviction difficult. The observer also noted that there was not a single German on the jury.[139]

The irate citizens were calmed only by the fact that Mundine was returned to jail and would soon stand trial for the murder of Mros. The district attorney, however, refused to prosecute Mundine again, presumably because he had no new evidence, and on May 5, 1886, the judge dismissed the case. Mundine went free until April 1899 when he was shot and killed by the Lexington constable, Cige Heffington.[140]

In contrast to the McDade lynching, the Thorndale lynching does not fit into the traditional pattern of vigilantism as described by Brown and illustrated by the McDade example. Thorndale had no gathering of the social elite to plan a course of action, there were no procedures that mimicked the legal procedures such as a trial, and a law enforcement process for Thorndale and Milam County was operational. But events in central Texas must be viewed as prologue because the vigilante tradition became part of the common history in the area and the concept of citizens taking matters into their own hands to obtain justice was incorporated into the mentality of the citizens of Lee and neighboring counties.

Even though the Thorndale lynching does not fit squarely into the pattern of traditional vigilantism it does approximate another variation of lynching outlined by Brown. Brown noted that in the second half of the nineteenth century Western vigilantism at times took place without the formal group of civic elite or the ritual-like procedure. The vigilante protocol had been implemented so frequently that it had become an abbreviated process. Adhering to the usual steps was time-consuming and that time could better be spent resolving the problem. Brown calls it *instant vigilantism*. So ingrained had the vigilante procedure become that it frequently functioned without organization or planning, and existed only for a single event. Instant vigilantism existed simultaneously with the traditional form. It was most commonly practiced in the West and could be racial, targeting Chinese residents. It was rarely used in the South against blacks.[141]

As a result of Thorndale's location in central Texas and the long history of conflict and violence, Thorndale's people were thoroughly familiar with vigilantism and were in a position to respond immediately to an anti-social act. Theirs was a single event and the justification was self-redress and retribution.

While Williamson and Lee counties provided the examples of the Western pattern for vigilantism, Milam County provided the setting for the Southern heritage and the lynch mob. Lynch mob violence became common in the South after the Civil War and generally targeted blacks. Once Reconstruction ended, the number of incidents declined, but beginning with Jim Crow legislation the numbers rose and for the period from 1882 to 1903 the number of blacks killed in the United States was more than 1,985.[142]

Although Tuskegee Institute and the *Chicago Tribune* both began keeping records of lynching, there was no formal, systematic mechanism for tabulating the number of people who lost their lives as a result of that act. More research on the local level would provide greater accuracy, but even without that the numbers are tragically high. Most of the deaths were in Southern states, and Texas ranked third, trailing Mississippi and Georgia. Of the 468 victims in Texas between 1885 and 1942, three hundred thirty-nine were black, seventy-seven were white, fifty-three were Hispanic, and one was an Indian. Half of the seventy-seven white victims were lynched in the mid- and late-1880s while more than half of Hispanics were killed in the twentieth century during the Mexican Revolution. For that same period from 1885 and 1942, forty percent of the mobs responded to instances of murder or attempted murder while only 26 percent resulted from the cases of rape or attempted rape.[143]

Even though Southern-type lynchings took place over several decades and in many different states, there were some hallmarks that helped identify the activity of lynch mobs. A significant feature was the presence of sadism and grizzly desecration and mutilation of the body. Intimidation and social control was part of the motivation and the barbarity helped to maximize the impact on African Americans. In addition to targeting primarily blacks, certain other features belonged to the pattern of the Southern lynch mob that was not often associated with vigilantism. Evidence for the alleged crime was generally flimsy, or even non-existent. Members of a mob were from the lower class although they had the tacit support of the community elite. The execution often included a man-hunt, torture, burning, or hanging. The event was planned and publicized so that people could travel from miles around to witness it. The spectators were numerous and in a festive mood, and the crowd included photographers who sold photos of the event. The participants of the lynching were readily identified, but the verdict by the coroner or his jury was that the victim died "at the hands of parties unknown." And resistance to the lynch mob by the officials was non-existent or minimal.[144]

One Milam County lynching, illustrating some of these features, would have been part of the Thorndale's collective memory. It took place on November 4, 1907, just four years prior to the Gomez lynching. Alex

Johnson, an African American, supposedly assaulted Miss Birdie Haley and "attempted to ravish her." The incident took place in Maysfield, eight miles northeast of Cameron. Acting quickly before a lynch mob could seize the suspect, the constable spirited Johnson away and brought him to the county jail in Cameron. The district court happened to be in session at the time and Judge J. C. Scott, who later would serve as judge in the first of the Thorndale cases, promised the citizens of Maysfield that there would be a speedy trial. The following Monday at ten o'clock, he convened a grand jury, and at the hearing Miss Haley identified Alex Johnson as the person who assaulted her. After listening to other evidence the grand jury, at about two o'clock, returned an indictment of assault and attempt to rape.

While the court was in session, about twenty-five men took places in and around the court house. When they heard the indictment and realized that the charge did not include the penalty of death, they headed for the jail with crowbars and sledge hammers. Judge Scott and others, including Maj. Richard Lyles, who would become a member of the defense team for the Thorndale men, spoke to the growing crowd and appealed to the people to permit the law to take its course. Their words had no effect.

The Milam County jail was one of the strongest in the state, and the members of the mob faced the obstacle of five steel doors before they could get to the cell holding Johnson. Guarding the prisoner were three armed men, the sheriff, John E. Holtzclaw, his deputy, and the jailer. They warned the mob that they would shoot the first man who attempted to enter the cell. The mob was not dissuaded and even threatened to use dynamite to blow up the jail. At 3:05 the mob entered the jail and the sheriff realized that his position was hopeless so he gave up the prisoner. The mob beat the victim just short of unconsciousness and then took him to a post oak tree on the west side of the courthouse and hanged him.[145]

The headline in the *Rockdale Reporter* read: **Negro Brute Hanged by a Crowd of Incensed Citizens.** The newspaper further identified the mob as "defenders of female virtue" and that the outraged public, "the highest tribunal. . . had tried, sentenced and executed this brute, thus meting out to him that punishment his crime deserved and which under the law he could not have received, as he was only indicted for the offense of assault with intent to rape." Four years later this same newspaper, but under new ownership, was critical of the Thorndale lynching. "No matter the circumstances leading up to this affair, Milam county [*sic*] must bow her head in shame over the horrible occurrence in our sister city ..." and it called on the governor to take drastic action in getting "to the bottom of the matter."[146]

The realization of the Cameron mob that a person indicted of a criminal act lesser than a capital crime, might avoid "proper" justice, was enough to motivate the mob to carry out a lynching. That same reasoning was present at the Thorndale after Zieschang was stabbed. While Zieschang was being attended to by a physician and while the constable took Gomez to the calaboose, the crowd on Main Street made no move to lynch anyone. When the word came that Zieschang died, they knew that Gomez would never be convicted of first degree murder because the crime had not been premeditated and he would face no more than a jail term. That is when the constable took Gomez out of the calaboose for protection and that is when some self-appointed men decided that it was necessary to kill Gomez before he could be taken to the county jail.

The Thorndale lynching was more of a Western lynching along the lines of instant vigilantism and less of a lynch mob of the Southern tradition. Some historians, as well as people living at the time of the lynching, projected their mental image of a Southern lynching on the Thorndale event and thereby accepted inaccuracies. Carrigan, in his study of lynching, stated: "In 1911, for example, a mob of a hundred Anglos beat, tortured, burned, and hanged a fourteen-year-old Mexican boy named Antonio Gomez in Thorndale, Texas. After murdering Gomez, the mob dragged his corpse through the streets of the town."[147]

The treatment of Gomez was brutal enough, but burning him and dragging the corpse through the streets of the town? There was no motivation for social control in the killing of Gomez. There were only about twenty-five people in the Mexican community to intimidate. If brutality, as exhibited in a Southern setting is indicative of racial hatred, then is it safe to conclude that if those aspects are not present, the actions at Thorndale were less a matter of race and more a matter of anger over the loss of a neighbor? The Thorndale lynching more closely approximates a Western lynching where the goal was a form of justice rather than the Southern act for social control.

Thorndale's heritage of violence belonged to the old mentality tugging Thorndale back to its past. The new Thorndale, with its business mentality, preferred to look to the future. Even the two victims illustrate this dualism.

Gomez, with ties to agriculture and hand labor, symbolized the past. Zieschang, with his commercial interest in automobiles and electricity, and his obsession with the town's image, symbolized the future. The Zieschang murder brought Thorndale back to the past and so did the lynching that followed.

V. THE ARRESTS
AND TRIALS

The arrest and trial of any person associated with a lynching was a rare occurrence in Texas. Carrigan and Webb wrote that when it came to the lynching of a Mexican "almost no white man was ever made to stand trial." Seldom, the authors maintained, did local and state officials even carry out investigations, and when they did, "they inevitably failed to identify those responsible."[148] The Thorndale lynching was therefore unusual in that four men were arrested and indicted, and three of them were tried. Assistant Attorney General C. E. Lane took pride in the arrests and said: "…for the first time in the history of a Texas lynching the supposed guilty persons have been arrested and placed in jail within four days after the lynching."[149]

Even Governor Oscar B. Colquitt, while congratulating the Milam County attorney for his efficiency, heralded it as an achievement and that "as many as four of the guilty parties" had been jailed. With a single exception, the governor could not recall any mob case within the previous twenty years that had been as successfully prosecuted as the Thorndale case.[150]

Instead of congratulating the county attorney, Colquitt should have congratulated himself, because it was he who had intervened and changed the case's direction. Everything that took place in Thorndale the day after the lynching, June 20, had followed the traditional pattern. In the event of an unusual death, the law required the local justice of the peace to conduct an inquest. The purpose of such an inquest would be to identify the cause of death and to learn about the conditions surrounding the death. If a coroner and not the justice of the peace conducted the inquest there would also have been a jury.[151] The frequent finding of coroners or justices of the peace when investigating Texas lynchings was that the victim had died by the "hands of persons unknown" and the case would be closed. If Colquitt had not intervened the Thorndale case would have been just another lynching case left unresolved. Once again citizens would have witnessed the failure of the Texas justice system to apprehend anyone associated with a lynching. The arrests on June 21 resulted from Colquitt's intervention.[152]

The method of intervention Colquitt selected was a court of inquiry. On June 21 Colquitt instructed Assistant Attorney General Lane and Texas State Ranger D. W. Cox to go to Cameron and initiate such a court. Most Americans associate a court of inquiry with military procedures and not with civilian cases. A court of inquiry, however, is part of the Texas legal system and resembles a grand jury that may be open to the public. Lane and Cox immediately departed from Austin by train and arrived at Cameron that same day. The next day, June 22, a court of inquiry reopened the Thorndale case, but this court of inquiry was held "behind closed doors."[153]

Without doubt Colquitt's decisive action stood in sharp contrast to the inactivity of earlier chief executives and deserves some analysis. Although Colquitt's motivation may have been purely altruistic and based solely on a desire of justice for all, there were also some political overtones. Colquitt had received the nomination in the Democratic primary of 1910, and in those days the winner of the Democratic primary was the sure winner of the election held on the first Tuesday in November. Not only had that primary been of critical importance for the November election, but there was also an issue: prohibition. Prohibition had been contested for some time and the opponents of prohibition, "the wets," had successfully blocked statewide prohibition. However, under the local option laws, many of the counties and portions of counties, had voted themselves "dry." The battle over prohibition had not ceased and the gubernatorial selection in the primary was one more skirmish in the conflict. Of the four Democrats, two of the candidates were in favor of prohibition and two candidates, one of which was Colquitt, were opposed to prohibition. Colquitt favored the use of local option that permitted the local jurisdiction to decide on the use of alcohol.

Even though no Texas citizen of Mexican descent was permitted to vote in Milam County Democratic primary, that exclusion was not the case in counties with large Tejano populations. As Catholics and imbibers, they, along with the Germans and Bohemians, were not part of the fundamentalist campaign against alcohol. Colquitt needed their votes, and the person who helped line up Mexican Americans in San Antonio, and also across the state, behind Colquitt was Francisco A. Chapa. Educated as a pharmacist at Tulane University, Chapa moved to San Antonio in 1890 and opened a drugstore. He also began publishing a newspaper titled *El Imparcial de Texas*. In addition to his successful business ventures he served on the city council, the school board, and the Fiesta Association. He gained the respect of the Mexican community and became a spokesman for its interests. Thanks in part to Chapa's support, Colquitt carried Bexar County by a impressive margin in the July Democratic primary. Colquitt received 4,301 votes while his three opponents totaled a mere 767. In the statewide tally, he won a solid plurality over his three opponents and went on to easily carry the November election. As governor, Colquitt made Chapa one of twelve advisors with the title of "lieutenant colonel." Chapa was the only Mexican American in the group.[154]

On June 21, 1911, Chapa, upon learning of the Thorndale incident, sent a telegram to Colquitt which read, "For the justice and humanity sake and for the fair name of Texas see that the criminals of Thorndale meet their just punishment." That same day Colquitt dispatched Lane and Cox to Cameron. Two days later Colquitt responded, addressing Chapa as "Dear Colonel," with a report of the actions already taken. Colquitt concluded with a promise that "[I] shall do what is in my power to bring these offenders to justice."[155]

Colquitt later credited an unnamed citizen of Milam County for his decision to intervene in the case, although Chapa's telegram must have carried some weight. Either way, the decision was politically astute. Newspapers throughout the state, in both the Anglo and Tejano communities, condemned the lynching. The *Dallas Times-Herald*, for example, called for the punishment of the "Thorndale mobites," while the *Beaumont Journal* laid ten to one odds that nothing would be done to them.[156] Even though lynching had been an accepted practice in the past, many citizens of Texas, by 1911, acknowledged the destructive nature of lynching to the nation.[157]

In the meantime, while the governor's intervention was taking shape, the news of Zieschang's death and the subsequent lynching of Gomez had flashed across the state by both telephone and telegraph. In Cameron, the sheriff of Milam County, A. D. Hooks, learned of the event and departed from Cameron the following day, June 20, and traveled to Thorndale to investigate.[158] No record has been found that describes his activity or his findings, so a reasonable assumption is that he made no arrests.

Even reports of an inquest are scarce. Only the *San Antonio Express* carried a statement made by Lane that so much as mentioned an inquest. In Lane's estimation the inquest had been "lax and defective and not at all in accordance with the regular methods pursued in such cases." But he said nothing more and there is no other information giving the location or date of an inquest or who directed it.[159]

There indeed had been an inquest. Woodbury Norris, twenty-eight years old, an insurance agent, and the Justice of the Peace for Precinct 8, Thorndale's precinct, had conducted an inquest on June 20. He interviewed two persons: Constable McCoy, who had been far removed from the scene of the crime, and Dr. Lovard Lee, who had examined the body. Norris later testified that he had sent his report to the county clerk's office in Cameron but he made no attempts to identify the wrong-doers because he thought it was not "any of my business." He assumed that the county officials would take care of the criminal investigation.[160]

Whether Norris's superficial inquest was a result of inexperience or an attempt to close the case, Lane's comment that the inquest was "lax" is valid. Perfunctory might be a better word. The Reverend J. L. Watson, a witness who later testified at the court of inquiry, stated that Norris encouraged him to say nothing. Norris denied telling anyone to remain silent.[161]

The court of inquiry met on June 22 and 23 (Thursday and Friday), in Cameron before the Justice of the Peace of Precinct No. 1, Ed English. Later both English and Lane claimed credit for the inquiry. Justice English, in a news release intended to correct "erroneous reports" that reflected negatively on citizens of Thorndale citizens, added that "Lane was present at the investigation ...." Lane, in a statement, intended to defend the governor against charges of indifference toward the lynching, claimed that he "conducted the court of inquiry assisted by Justice of the Peace Ed English."[162]

The court heard testimony from thirty-seven witnesses and at the end of the Thursday session Justice English issued warrants for the arrests of four Thorndale citizens. The *Express* reporter observed that the Thorndale citizens who were in Cameron seemed to deplore the lynching and desired punishment of the perpetrators.[163]

The Mexican consul in San Antonio, Miguel E. Diebold, upon reading of the lynching in the newspaper, dispatched the vice-consul, Eduardo Velardo, to collect information and observe the judicial procedures. Velardo boarded the next train and arrived at Thorndale on the twenty-second at one o'clock in the morning. He took a room in Thorndale's hotel, which he found somewhat shabby (*de mala aparienca*). In the morning, after breakfast, he examined the crime scene and interviewed several Anglos and also a Mexican who owned a small shop. He then traveled by train to Cameron and attended the court of inquiry. Upon his return to San Antonio, Velardo reported to Diebold, and Diebold in turn sent a report to the Mexican Embassy in Washington. In contrast to laudatory comments by Lane and English, the Mexican officials were not satisfied with events in Milam County. Only four men had been arrested even though testimony implicated at least twenty-five citizens. So great was the Mexican dissatisfaction with Texas officials that the Mexican government considered filling a complaint with the State Department.[164]

On June 24, Diebold asked Colquitt for a copy of the records of the court of inquiry and expressed his certitude that county and state officials would do everything permitted by law to punish the guilty persons. Colquitt sent a copy of the testimony on June 26, along with a bill for $7.50 for transcription costs, and reassured Diebold of his intent to enforce the law.[165]

In adherence to English's arrest orders, Sheriff Hooks returned to Thorndale on Thursday, traveling by auto, and arrived that evening at six o'clock. The four men named in the orders, Z. T. Gore, Jr., Ezra Stephens, Garrett Noack, and Harry Wuensche, gave themselves up that night, and Friday noon (June 23) they and the sheriff left for Cameron on the 12:38 P.M. train.[166]

Even though the four men were in custody and calm prevailed in Thorndale, a primary witness at the hearing, Wilford Wilson, worried about his own and his family's security. Instead of telephoning Lane about his concern, Wilson wrote a letter because he suspected that the telephone operators would listen to his conversation and then spread the news that Wilson was uneasy. Wilson's concern arose when he observed four mounted men slowly riding back and forth in front of his house without speaking to each other. Wilson suspected that the purpose of their action was intimidation and he requested some Rangers to be dispatched to Thorndale. Lane forwarded Wilson's letter to Colquitt and in keeping with the "one riot-one Ranger" mystique of the Rangers, Colquitt dispatched a single "capable and trusty" member of the Ranger Force.[167]

Colquitt, sensitive to the feelings of the local law officers over jurisdictional infringement, sent a letter to Sheriff Hooks notifying him of the Ranger's presence and solicited Hook's response to the governor's action. Hooks responded that Rangers were not necessary because "things were quiet and everything [was] moving along nicely."[168]

The next step in the judicial process took place a week later on July 3 (Monday) with an examining trial. The four men who were charged were brought before Justice English at ten o'clock. The four appeared for a few minutes and were then returned to the county jail. The attorneys for both the defense and the prosecution agreed to argue the case on the evidence gathered by the court of inquiry. English refused the request to grant bail and the attorneys for the defendants announced their intention to sue for a writ of habeas corpus with District Judge J. C. Scott.[169]

On July 31 (Monday) at the habeas corpus hearing, Judge Scott, in a special session of the district court, rejected bail for three of the accused, but granted Gore bail in the sum of $4,000. No records of the proceedings have been found and no reason for granting bail to one but not the others was recorded. Eleven Thorndale men, including Gore's father, and G. W. Penny, owner of the house where Gomez had been briefly hidden, were the sureties.[170]

The Milam County grand jury met on October 24 (Tuesday) and returned indictments for murder in the first degree against all four. A special venire for ninety men was then issued for each case with instructions to appear at Cameron on November 6. Each of the accused was to be tried separately. A request for a change of venue was denied so the trial was scheduled for Cameron on Monday November 6, 1911, in the district court presided by Judge Scott.[171]

The first to be tried was Z. T. (Taylor) Gore, Jr. Gore was the twenty-two-year-old son of a retired farmer. Sometime between 1874 and 1880 the Gore family moved from Kentucky to Texas and in 1900 the elder Gore owned an un-mortgaged farm in Milam County. By 1910 he had sold the farm and the family lived in a rented house in Thorndale. During the forty-one years of marriage his wife, Mildred Gore, had given birth to thirteen children, but only five survived. Two of the children, a son, Junior, and a daughter lived with the parents. Gore, Jr. had been born in Thorndale on July 14, 1888, but neither he nor his younger sister was employed in 1910. Seven years later, in 1917, when he registered for military service, he gave his occupation as a farmer, and he was described as a person of medium height with a slender build, blue eyes, and light brown hair. The card also stated that he had a crippled ankle.[172]

The State was represented by W. C. Davis of Bryan, Assistant Attorney General Lane of Austin, and W. A. Morrison of Cameron. Gore was represented by Cameron lawyers T. S. Henderson and Maj. Richard Lyles, a seventy-one-year-old veteran of the Civil War, and G. L. Perkinson of Thorndale.

In the preliminary arguments, which began on November 4, the attorneys debated the age and size of Gomez. The prosecution claimed that Gomez was about thirteen years old and weighed less than fifty pounds—"a wizened little figure." The defense countered that he was nineteen years old and though he was undersized, he was capable of a man's actions when he stabbed Zieschang. Justice English issued a statement of facts that he had developed as a result of the court of inquiry. He estimated that about twenty witnesses from Thorndale would be asked to testify.[173]

Obtaining the requisite number of men for the jury of twelve from the venire of ninety men was not possible, so a second call went out for fifty more candidates. At the end of the session on November 8 (Wednesday) jury selection had not been completed, so the judge ordered a third venire of fifty men. Officials rode nearly all night summoning potential jurors. Finally, on November 9, the jury was seated and began listening to testimony.[174]

The next day, November 10, the first witness, Wilford Wilson, testified. He had been the primary witness at the court of inquiry and was the person who had requested Ranger protection. Wilson was thirty years old, and, because he was a rural mail carrier, was widely known. His use of a motorcycle in delivering the mail was symbolic of his modern outlook on life. As a teenager he had helped string the telephone line from Taylor to Hearn, and when electricity was available in Thorndale, he installed electrical wire in the Woodmen of the World Opera House.[175]

No court transcript of Wilson's testimony has been found. A correspondent for the *San Antonio Express*, however, was in attendance and sent his report to the newspaper the day of the trial. The discrepancies in Wilson's testimony before the court of inquiry and his testimony at the trial could well be the result of the reporter's errors. According to Wilson's testimony at the trial, Constable McCoy placed Gomez under Wilson's charge and asked him to fasten a trace chain with a lock around Gomez's neck and keep him secure. McCoy then departed in order to obtain an auto and instructed Wilson to meet him at a neighboring church with the prisoner. However, McCoy was not at the church at the appointed time, so Wilson took Gomez to the residence of G. W. Penny. From him Wilson learned that the owner of the auto was out of town and McCoy had gone to find another auto.

Shortly after Wilson and Gomez entered Penny's house, four men appeared at Penny's house and asked if the boy was inside. It was too dark to see the men's faces, but Wilson recognized the men by their voices. After a few minutes Wilson took Gomez out of the house through a rear door and into the alley. There the two were intercepted by four men who tried to grab Gomez. Gomez avoided them by running around Wilson, using Wilson as a shield. Finally, near the end of the alley a man on horseback rushed his horse between Wilson and the boy, grasped the chain and galloped down the street, dragging the boy by the chain. The others, including Wilson, all followed at a run. When Wilson caught up, the men were at a telephone pole[176] on Main Street with the boy lying on the ground gasping for air. Wilson raised the boy's head to the sidewalk and one of the men kicked the boy's head. When other men came up, Wilson left the scene. He returned later and found Gomez hanging on the pole by the trace chain. Penny was the second witness and he generally corroborated Wilson's testimony.[177]

Although the indictment had been for murder in the first degree, the jury instructions provided five options. The first option of murder in the first degree carried with it the death sentence or life imprisonment. To convict the jury needed to be convinced beyond a reasonable doubt that Gore, "with malice aforethought" formed a design to kill and did so by dragging Gomez on the ground with a chain fastened around his neck, then striking him on the head with some form of instrument, and finally hanging him by the chain attached around his neck.

A second alternative was murder in the second degree which carried with it a prison sentence of not less than five years. The act of murder remained the same, but instead of malice aforethought being proven; the jury needed to believe that there was implied malice, malice demonstrated from the act, but malice that could not be proven.

A third option was to deliver a verdict of murder in the first degree if Gore, even though he may not have physically touched the victim, knew of the planned intent to murder and encouraged the persons who, with *express* malice, were actually engaged in the act. If the jury was convinced that Gore had assisted Stephens, Noack, and Wuensche by keeping watch for anyone who might interrupt the murder, he would be guilty.

The fourth charge was murder in the second degree if the other persons were guilty of murder with *implied* malice and Gore was present and encouraged the act, even if he did not actually physically assist. He would also be guilty if he served as a look-out while the act was perpetrated.

The last choice was a finding of not guilty if the jury believed that Gore, although present at the unlawful act, was not aware of the intent, did not assist or encourage the murder, or was indeed absent. Circumstantial evidence could not be used as a basis for conviction unless each fact used to lead to such a conclusion, was be proven beyond a reasonable doubt.[178]

While the instructions for the jury were largely legal boilerplate, a specific charge brought against Gore and not the others in subsequent trials, was that Gore kept watch in order to prevent any "interruption" in the killing of Gomez by the other three. The alleged role as sentinel may have been related to restricted mobility resulting from the crippled foot reported in 1917.

On November 11, Gore testified on his own behalf and presented his alibi. He acknowledged that he had been at Penny's gate the night of the lynching. He had heard that Gomez had been detained at the house and went there out of curiosity. He denied participating in the rush on the prisoner and insisted that he did not hear any whistle signal. Instead he had returned to his own home from Penny's house and en route had encountered Grover Williams. Gore later returned to town after the death of Gomez. He denied seeing any of the other three accused that night. During cross examination he admitted that he had been with Ezra Stephens, one of the defendants, after Zieschang's stabbing. Then Gore and Stephens had driven out of town with two other persons and had walked back. The jury deliberated for approximately one hour and acquitted Gore after the first ballot.[179] Upon hearing the verdict Gore's friends, sympathizers, and influential people of Thorndale "gave loud and tumultuous shouts of applause and clapping of hands and demonstrations commendatory of the act of said jury...."[180]

Immediately after the verdict of innocence, Davis, attorney for the State, applied for a change of venue for the remaining three cases. After extensive arguments, Judge Scott, on November 17, granted the request and transferred the three remaining cases to Williamson County. Sheriff Hooks and his deputy escorted the three men to Georgetown and the Williamson County jail.[181]

In the meantime, the attorneys for the defense had filed a brief that appealed Judge Scott's refusal to release the three defendants on bail. Two months later, on January 31, the Texas Court of Criminal Appeals rendered its decision upholding Judge Scott's ruling. The judges reasoned that the evidence of the case warranted a conviction of first degree murder and they would not overturn Scott's decision unless they were convinced that Scott was holding the wrong persons. The three accused therefore remained in the Williamson County jail to await their trials.[182]

The second person to face trial was Garrett P. Noack. At the age of thirty-two, Noack was the oldest of the four men who had been arrested. His given name was actually Gerhardt, but when non-Germans heard his name pronounced by a German, it sounded like Garrett. His parents were part of the Wendish community and had migrated to Texas in 1877 just before his birth in 1879. His two brothers and his two sisters, one of whom was adopted, had been born in Germany. Two more siblings, a sister and a brother, were born in Texas. In 1883 the father of seven died and the widowed mother managed the family alone for three years, when she remarried. In 1900, when Garrett was twenty-one, he was living in Fayette County and worked as a laborer on his brother's farm. In November 1902 he was in Thorndale and campaigned for the position of constable for Beat 8. He ran as an Independent and he lost to the Democrat by six votes. His mother also moved to Thorndale and died there in 1903.[183]

In April 1910 he became the agent for the City Brewery of San Antonio, and one of his first tasks was to place a notice in the newspaper asking "all parties who have empty kegs belonging to this brewery to please bring them in."[184] Hoping to supplement his income he acquired a full-blooded Jersey bull, charging $2.50 for the service and guaranteed a calf. Garrett married in 1906 and by 1910 he was the father of two boys, Willie and John. A third son was born in May 1911, just a month before the lynching.[185]

Noack's trial began on February 26, 1912, (Monday) in Georgetown. C. A. Wilcox was the district judge. District Attorney J. R. Hamilton and Lane represented the State and the attorneys for the defense were Major Lyles of Cameron, Perkinson of Thorndale, J. F. Taulbee, and Judge T. J. Lawhon of the Williamson county bar. G. E. Grider, an attorney from San Antonio, had been employed by the Mexican government to observe the trial, to ensure that the case was actively prosecuted, and that there was compliance with all forms of the law.

The same day as the beginning of the trial, Monday, a special train carrying Noack's friends and prospective witnesses departed from Thorndale, stopped at Taylor where some more passengers climbed aboard, and brought about 150 men to Georgetown. They remained in Georgetown for the duration of the trial.[186]

The problem of seating a jury was as great in Williamson County as it had been in Milam. Three consecutive venires summoning first sixty, then forty, and finally twenty men had been issued and not until nine o'clock on Tuesday night was the jury sworn in. Most men would have been declared eligible under the usual standards, but many were rejected on the question of race prejudice. Potential jurors were asked if they believed that the same legal standards that applied in the trial of a white man for killing a Mexican would be equally valid if the races were reversed. The Georgetown journalist feared that the "county would have to be raked over to find the qualified jurors."[187] Although the newspapers reporting the Gore trial did not mention that the same question had been asked of jurors in Cameron, in all likelihood it had been, and presented the same stumbling block.

The State began examining witnesses on Wednesday, February 28, and rested its case at six that evening. None of the witnesses identified Noack as one of the actual lynchers, and all of the evidence presented by the state was circumstantial. On Thursday the defense introduced a request to withdraw from consideration all evidence admitted on the theory that Noack had entered into a conspiracy to kill Gomez. There was no proof that Noack had seen, spoken to, or had a conversation with the three accused, and there was no proof that he raised his hand to injure Gomez, or assisted or encouraged others to take the life of Gomez. Wilson testified that Noack had been at the Penny house and near the telephone post, but he did not see Noack take any action or hear him say anything in the nature of a threat. Noack denied being at the Penny house or at the crime scene and stated that he had been at the Bank Saloon, in an office above the Bank Saloon, and near the train depot. He did admit that when he had been in front of the Bank Saloon, and that he had cursed upon hearing that Gomez had been removed from Thorndale, but he denied that it had been a threat or part of a conspiracy.[188]

The instructions to the jury in the Noack case included the same first three charges given to Gore's jury: murder in the first degree, murder in the second degree, and being present at the crime and encouraging or aiding the participants, The fourth charge differed from charges in the previous trial and focused on conspiracy to commit the crime. Any person who conspired to commit the crime would be treated as a principal in the act. The jury instructions also spelled out what constituted a conspiracy. To be found guilty of conspiracy there must be evidence that Noack made a "positive agreement" with one or more persons to commit murder, that he was aware of the unlawful intent, and that he encouraged the crime with words or gestures. The jury began deliberations on March 1, 1912, (Friday), and within twenty minutes it returned the verdict of not guilty. Noack had been in jail for nine months.[189]

The third person to be tried was twenty-two-year old Ezra A. Stephens. His father, William S. Stephens, originated from Georgia and at the turn of the century he owned the Golden Rule Saloon in Thorndale. Later he formed a partnership and became part-owner of the Blue Front Saloon.

In October 1910 the partners moved their saloon into the former bank building and named their establishment the Old Bank Saloon. The owners provided cold beer, high-proof bonded "whiskies" and "fine wines for sacramental purposes."[190] He also owned a house in Thorndale and it was not mortgaged. Ezra, the couple's only child, lived with them. He had been employed as a bookkeeper with the German Mercantile Company, a dry goods store, but gave up the position in September 1910 when he and Oscar Schiller opened a land and insurance company. Their office occupied the front room of the second floor above the Bank Saloon. Stephens was active on Thorndale's social scene and was engaged to be married.[191]

Ezra A. Stephens.
Courtesy of Roy H. Zieschang

Postcard sent from Mrs. William
Stephens to her son in jail.
The reverse side of the card carries the photograph
of Zieschang on the day of his death shown in
the first chapter. *Courtesy of Roy H. Zieschang*

Stephens' trial began on April 29 (Monday) with jury selection. Again the crucial test for the jurors was the question of race prejudice. By noon Tuesday the requisite number of jurors was secured and the examination of witnesses began. On Wednesday, May 1, at ten o'clock, the state rested and the court recessed so the defense could consult with the witnesses and prepare for the afternoon session.[192]

The trial resumed on Thursday (May 2) and continued on until10:20 Thursday night when the jury acquitted Stephens. The decision to acquit was made after two ballots, and deliberation consumed forty minutes. Two jurors had voted for conviction on the first ballot. About two hundred friends and supporters had come for the decision by a special train from Thorndale and scores more had been in Georgetown all week. The audience had been warned against any demonstration when the decision was announced, and there was none. When Stephens heard the acquittal, he turned and kissed his mother and she leaned her head against his breast and patted his cheek. Stephens then walked to the jury box and shook hands with each juror and thanked him. Stephens was immensely popular in Thorndale, and shortly after his return to Thorndale, on May 12, he married Myrle Locklin, his fiancée.[193]

Within a few moments after Stephens' acquittal, Wuensche's counsel applied for his release on bail. Judge Wilcox granted it setting the amount a $5,000. Thorndale people rushed forward to sign the document until it was filled with names. With the release of Wuensche the Thorndale residents headed for the train, which departed Georgetown late that night and arrived at Thorndale at 2 o'clock the next morning. Nearly the entire town was at the station and welcomed its arrival. The defendants were viewed as martyrs after having been incarcerated for nearly a year and accumulating legal fees of slightly less than $10,000.[194]

Although out on bail, Harry C. Wuensche still faced trial. Wuensche was twenty-two-years-old, married, and a father. His grandfather and great-grandfather had crossed the Atlantic on the *Ben Nevis* in 1854. Following the pattern of many of the Wends who lived in Thorndale, the family first settled in the Serbin community, then farmed near Fedor, and finally moved to Thorndale in the mid-1880s. Harry's father, John Charles "Charlie" Wuensche, worked as a farmer in 1900 and in 1910 he managed a lumberyard. He had married Mary Lehmann in 1888 and by 1910 there were eight children, with Harry being the eldest, born in November 1888. When Harry was twenty-one he married Beulah Williams, described in the newspaper as "quite young, being only 'sweet sixteen' and very pretty." Harry was identified as "a very popular and promising young man."[195]

At the time of the marriage Harry had a position in the clothing department of Smith-Bunting but later that year, when the census enumerator made his rounds, Harry was working as a clerk in a grocery stone. The young couple lived in a house that they owned, and supplemented their income by boarding a young man who worked in a dry goods store. By September Harry held yet another position and the newspaper reported that "the hustling grocery boy is now engaged in 'passing schooners over the bar' at the Blue Front Saloon."[196]

Near the end of December Harry became the proud father of a ten-and-one-half pound baby girl. For Charles Wuensche, the grandfather, it was a happy event and his friends presented him with "a nice gold cane." For the maternal grandfather, Ben F. Williams, the birth was less eventful—it was his sixteenth grandchild. Harry was separated from his young family for almost a year, but at least once, during his incarceration in Cameron, his young wife traveled to the county seat for a visit of several days.[197]

On the first Monday in June Judge Wilcox, on the motion of the District Attorney, removed Harry Wuensche's case from the docket. A newspaper reporter observed that the last three defendants had been denied bail and had been in jail for nearly a year, "so they were pretty severely punished after all."[198]

Guilty or Not ?

The Thorndale lynching was not a typical lynching. It was spontaneous, quickly executed, without extensive discussion or planning. The number of men involved was small and done while the "mob" of a hundred or more was a block away, south of the railroad tracks, unaware of the actual lynching. It was done at about ten o'clock at night, three hours after sunset. Visibility was limited and some identification was based on physical size and voice recognition. There was no desecration of the body and no photographs of citizens standing next to the dangling corpse, and no festive crowd. A Thorndale resident, ten days after the event, hesitated to draw any conclusions because every person he talked with told a different version.[199]

Detailing the events and identifying the perpetrators was hampered by these unusual conditions, and news reporters filled in the gaps by projecting the Thorndale event over the standard lynching pattern. As a result some stereotypical features of the usual lynching as well as some false assumptions seeped into the newspaper accounts. For example, "...a mob of at least one hundred men prominent in the county, formed in a mass and proceeding to the jail, broke down the door...." "Twenty men ran for ropes, but the mob was too impatient to wait." "Dozens of hands grasped the chain ...." [200]

Given the unique aspects of the act, a reasonable topic for speculation is the guilt or innocence of the four who were arrested and charged. It is natural to conclude that a person who has been indicted of a crime was also guilty. But one must also remember that a competent prosecutor can generally persuade a grand jury to bring an indictment. Or, as it is stated on occasion, "He could get the grand jury to indict a ham sandwich." The grand jury's indictment for first degree murder was hardly a reasonable charge and yet the grand jury voted for it. Moreover, an indictment merely states that there is enough evidence to warrant a jury trial.

One can also be misled by previous, supposedly typical, jury decisions, which failed to convict, and assume that identical logic applied to the Thorndale trials. In some cases the person charged with murder had not been found guilty simply because of the circumstances surrounding the crime. No jury at that time in Texas, for example, would convict anyone who found his wife in bed with another man and then emptied both barrels of his twelve-gauge shotgun into the two of them. It is also easy to assume that a jury would rarely convict anyone who killed a murderer, especially in this case since Gomez was clearly the one who killed Zieschang. It is possible that the juries in both counties looked at the lynching as an act that was justified by Zieschang's murder. Following established legal procedures Gomez would never have been charged with murder in the first degree, the only charge that carried the death sentence, because his was an impulsive act. But he had taken a life and most citizens would think he needed to pay with his life.

Could it be that racial prejudice against Mexicans was so great among the jurors that avenging the death of a Mexican was not worth imprisoning anyone, much less executing or imprisoning four young white men? The prosecution was aware of racial prejudice and its potential in the decision, and made it part of their questioning of prospective jurors. Assuming that jury selection was effective and that the jurors did not lie about their views about equality under the law, racial prejudice should have been kept at a minimum.

While all of these possibilities might have prevented the conviction of the four suspects even though they were guilty, it is also possible that the case was weak and that the prosecution failed to prove the defendants committed the crime. Strategies followed by prosecuting attorneys may vary, but when four dependents are tried separately, the logic would be to begin with the strongest case and obtain a conviction so that the momentum would carry through in the subsequent cases. The weakness of the prosecution's cases is evident when the second case, theoretically their second strongest, was based solely on circumstantial evidence.

When the jury found the first defendant not guilty the prosecutors asked for a change of venue. If the first case was indeed their strongest, and they could not get a conviction on it, then their only hope for a conviction on a weaker case would be a change of venue.

The evidence presented by the prosecution was not compelling, a problem for even the most gifted prosecutor. Motive, a vital element in most trials, was not a consideration. Revenge was the motive and it could fit any number of people in Thorndale not just those four. Positive identification was another problem. There were no witnesses who were at the scene of the crime when the body was hoisted. The defendants had alibis, which admittedly can be fabricated, but there was cross examination.

The Georgetown journalist believed that the trials were expensive farces. A Mexican had killed a popular citizen and his friends arose and avenged the death. There never was a chance of a conviction and there would never be a similar situation in the future. "Reasonable doubt," he wrote, won another victory.[201] So the finding of not guilty does not necessarily exempt the four defendants, but neither can we conclude that they were guilty.

One, or all four, may indeed have been innocent. There were forces at work which may have led to false arrests. State officials, such as the governor, and civic leaders in Thorndale and Milam County were acutely cognizant of their electorate and public pressure may have been great enough to compel them to rapid action instead of careful investigation leading to the actual culprits. The pressure on Governor Colquitt to act came from both the citizens and from the Mexican government. Texas officials may have been cynical enough to believe that no jury would convict anyone involved in a lynching, so even if an innocent person were tried, he would not be convicted. Speedy investigations, arrests, and trials would bring an end to the public outcry for ferreting out the perpetrators. Taking pride in making arrests within four days, which the Assistant Attorney General did, is less impressive than taking a month to arrest the persons identified by solid evidence.

And there was the matter of civic image and the civic shame brought on the county and town. The *San Antonio Express* stated "The majority of the mob are men well known in Milam County, some known throughout the state." Justice English said that the "best citizens of Thorndale" testified to the court. "The spirit of mob violence must be curbed, and the Thorndale disgrace should be thoroughly sifted."[202] Rapid action would dispel those allegations and normal life could resume.

The *Thorndale Thorn* argued that the other newspapers that were critical of Thorndale should have withheld their criticism until they knew more about the Thorndale citizens who are as "honest, fair-minded and law abiding" as any in the state. A committee of Thorndale citizens sent a letter complaining that the press had not reported the incident correctly and instead sent its own version of the murder and lynching. It was a condensed version, with the abusive language removed, and expressed their regret over the entire affair.[203] Hasty prosecution would silence the critics in other towns.

Officials should have taken more time to resolve conflicting details given at the court of inquiry and the actual jury trials. And those little details were not inconsequential. Wilson, the primary witness, told the court of inquiry that he went to obtain an automobile, but while testifying at Gore's trial he said that McCoy had gone for the auto. Whoever went for the auto was gone for more than an hour. Did Wilson follow the four men as they ran toward the telephone pole, or did the men run toward the east while he went south to town to get help? And there were conflicting statements between witnesses. Did McCoy and Wilson take Gomez to the gin, about one hundred yards away from the calaboose, as McCoy said, or did Wilson accompany the other two a short distance and then search for a car was Wilson testified?

Also, why did not Penny and Wilson simply hide Gomez and then tell the men that they had not seen him? Penny told them that Gomez was in his house. Why did Wilson take Gomez out the back door? McCoy had told Wilson to remove Gomez from the Penny house if he could not withstand the mob. But the mob never even entered Penny's yard gate and when Wilson warned them not to make trouble and advised them to leave, they left. Even more puzzling was the absence of Constable McCoy. Why did he not remain with his prisoner? He was responsible for the prisoner and Thorndale was not so large that his search for a car would have taken him away from the place he should have been. He removed Gomez from the calaboose at about eight o'clock and the final acts of the lynching were at about ten o'clock.

That a lynching occurred is not in question, but no one should conclude that the four charged with the murder were the perpetrators or that the justice system failed by not finding them guilty. The system failed to find those who were guilty, and given the circumstances peculiar to this lynching, proving the charges might well have been impossible. In this single instance a finding that a person died "by the hands of parties unknown" would have been accurate.

VI. THE MEXICAN CONTEXT

Racial Prejudice in Milam County

In the land of black and white the Mexican was white—at least in the census. Census enumerators who filled in the square under "Color or Race" used "W" for white, "B" for black, and "M" not for Mexican but for mulatto. Mexicans and Mexican Americans were identified as "W." On occasion an enumerator wrote "ol" for individuals presumably meaning "olive." In order to identify a Mexican it is necessary to look under a different census column: "Place of birth."

Even though the enumerators classified Mexicans as white, the item on the census asking race or color supports the thought that color could well be significant. A truism for African Americans in that era held that being mulatto was preferable to being black. Is it safe to assume that being olive-skinned was also an advantage over black? One scholar disagrees and states that the whites "regarded Mexicans as a colored people, discerned the Indian ancestry in them, and identified them socially with blacks."[204]

Another study, instead of generalizing that a view of whites toward Mexicans was the same across the state, pointed out that Mexicans in central Texas were not subjected to the same kind of abuse as those living in the Rio Grande Valley. William Carrigan in his study of lynching in central Texas chose seven counties for close examination. "There is only one documented case of mob violence against a Mexican in the seven central Texas counties at the heart of this study." He concluded that there was less prejudice against Mexicans in central Texas than in the

Rio Grande Valley because Mexicans were needed as workers to replace the blacks who had been driven out by the violence against them. And Mexicans worked for lower wages than other workers. However, when he refers to the Gomez lynching, he incorrectly places Milam County in southern Texas when in actual fact Milam County is in central Texas adjoining Bell and Falls counties, two of the seven counties he examined. Even if the Gomez lynching is counted as a central Texas incident, his point that there was less violence against Mexicans in central Texas than in the Valley may have validity.[205]

Assuming that the level of prejudice and discrimination against Mexicans in central Texas was as Carrigan stated, another possible explanation for that difference could be the sparse population of Mexicans in central Texas. The number of Mexicans in the Thorndale precinct was small, especially when compared to Negroes. There were 265 blacks and thirty-seven mulattos in the precinct and only forty-five Mexicans and persons of Mexican descent. Even though the practices or procedures of segregation had been institutionalized for blacks, formalizing a system for the Mexicans may have reached diminishing returns for the few Mexicans. Vice-consul Eduardo Velardo, for example, obtained a room in Thorndale's hotel—something that would not have happened with a black. No matter how shabby, residential options necessary for implementing segregation for Mexicans were limited.

And the 1910 census lists a family in Thorndale's precinct in which a Texan of German descent was married to a woman, born in Texas, of Mexican descent. The couple had been married for twenty-seven years and had ten children. Miscegenation between whites and blacks, on the other hand, was illegal.[206]

Although of small comfort to Antonio Gomez, the abusive language directed toward him as he was whittling, such as "little son-of-a bitch" or "I will whip his damned ass," was not racial, but racially-neutral billingsgate used for whites as well. And the bar keeper, Stephens, engaged Antonio in play-like scuffling to keep emotions from rising. The issue was not Antonio's presence, but his actions.

Even if the walls of separation were not as high for Mexicans as they were for blacks, the census does hint at some segregation between Mexicans and whites. A large number of the Mexicans in Milam Country worked in the coal mines near Rockdale[207] and Mexican names are generally not interspersed with Anglo names, but are grouped. The same is true for the Thorndale precinct where ten Mexicans worked for the railroad and lived in the house rented by the Mexican foreman. However, that type of segregation may be more related to occupation, language, and culture than race.

Another hint of discrimination in the census may be occupation, in that Mexicans were laborers and not professionals or merchants—although Velardo interviewed a Mexican store owner in Thorndale. But that evidence also may again be related to language proficiency or economic decisions rather than race. The Mexican workers were generally young men, without families, who were part of the transient labor force. Gabriel Gamez, Antonio's father, although in the transient labor force, was a family man and an exception to the rule.

Mexicans, therefore, may well have enjoyed less discrimination than blacks, and Mexicans may have been treated better in central Texas than in the Rio Grande Valley, but prejudice, whether because of color or culture, existed. The most convincing evidence for the existence of prejudice was the difficulty in the selection of the juries in both Milam and Williamson counties. In both places three repeated calls for jurors were necessary to find the requisite twelve men. In Milam County 140 were summoned and in Williamson County it took 120, leading an editor to wonder if was necessary to "rake over" the entire county to find qualified jurors. The stumbling block was the question asked of each candidate by the state's attorneys: "Are the same legal standards applied in the trial of a white man for killing a Mexican as would be were the races reversed?" The fact that the attorneys asked the question and that so many men were disqualified, documents the existence of discriminatory views toward Mexicans.[208]

And finally, in the political arena separation was starkly clear. Beginning in 1903 the Texas Legislature passed a minor law that culminated twenty years later in an instrument of disenfranchisement known as the white primary. Following the passage of that minor law, the Democratic Party's executive committee notified the counties' leaders that they could require a voter in the party primary to avow that he was a white person and a Democrat. Although blacks were the target of the policy and the state leaders preferred to define persons of Mexican descent as white, they authorized the county officials to specify who was to be counted as white. The Milam County Democrats interpreted "white" narrowly, and in a newspaper notice they informed the citizens that voting in the Thorndale Democratic primary was strictly for white men, and that excluded "negroes, Mexicans, and all other persons [presumably women] except white men."[209]

The Role of the Mexican Government

Nations are not only responsible for the welfare of citizens living in the homeland but also for their citizens or countrymen living in other nations. Diplomats intervene if their citizens are abused or need assistance. But who speaks for a minority when a nation abuses its own minority? Jews, for example, had no homeland early in the twentieth century, and some believed the holocaust would not have happened if there had been a Jewish nation. The formation of Israel in 1948 was justified in part as a guarantee that it would never happen again. Blacks in America were in a situation similar to that of Jews before the formation of Israel. They were subject to the laws of the country in which they were citizens, but if that country deprived them of their rights, no foreign nation would call the United States to account. Antonio Gomez was born in Texas and was therefore a citizen of the United States and not a Mexican national. To what extent was the Mexican government obligated to respond?

Twenty years prior to the Thorndale lynching, in 1891, eleven Italians in New Orleans were lynched. The police chief in New Orleans had been killed, gangland style, immediately before he was expected to go public with information about the presence of the Mafia in the city. After a trial, which found the accused Sicilians not guilty of the crime, citizens broke into the jail and shot or hanged all eleven. Italy protested, even though some of the eleven had become American citizens, and after negotiations failed, Italy broke diplomatic relations with the United States. The diplomatic controversy continued for two years before it was resolved.[210]

The problem a foreign government faced in obtaining satisfaction for past injuries to its citizens in the United States or to prevent injuries from occurring was federalism. The central government controlled diplomacy, but the state and local governments were responsible for law enforcement on the level where the abuses took place. Violence against another person was a state offense and the county or state courts were jurisdictionally responsible. So while the Mexicans on the local scene could not get satisfaction from Texas justice, neither were the results any better if they brought their grievances to the Mexican government.

Further complicating diplomatic efforts in the protection of Mexicans in the United States was the turmoil in Mexico during the first two decades of the twentieth century. Throughout much of the previous century Mexico had suffered from military defeat, unstable governments, and economic backwardness. Finally, in 1876, Porfirio Díaz brought greater centralization and order to the nation with a firm hand. But his concept of order and stability came at a high personal price for opponents and many faced death or imprisonment. Often the opponents found safety in Texas or along Mexico's northern border. Díaz's order and stability provided a suitable environment for economic growth and European and American investors provided the stimulus for industrialization. But his approach also had a trade-off and could be considered as nothing more than an enticement to foreign capitalists to exploit Mexico's natural resources. Until 1910 his re-elections were closely managed and Díaz maintained his presidency. In 1910, however, the popularity of an opponent, Francisco I. Madero, grew and on June 6, 1910, Díaz found it necessary to imprison him. Madero was bailed out of prison and like many others fled to Texas for his safety. Díaz proclaimed his own re-election and was clinging to office when the Rock Springs lynching took place in Texas.[211]

Antonio Rodríguez, age twenty or twenty-three, was killed on November 3, 1910, at Rock Springs, Edwards County, in western Texas. He had been arrested and charged with the murder of an Anglo American woman. While he was awaiting trial a mob removed him from the jail, and tied him to a mesquite tree. Every man in the mob became a participant by tossing a tree branch around Rodríguez. They then poured on some kerosene and burned him. The verdict of the coroner's jury found that "an unknown Mexican met death at the hands of an unknown mob," and no arrests were made.[212]

As the news spread in Mexico, riots broke out in several cities including Mexico City and Guadalajara where the rioters attacked Americans living in Mexico and property owned by Americans. Part of the motivation was resentment of American racism, arrogance, and economic exploitation of Mexican resources. But both Díaz and his opponents encouraged the demonstrations. Díaz hoped that the increased severity of the demonstrations in Texas would lead to a crack-down by American authorities on Díaz opponents who had escaped to Texas, while the anti-Díaz group saw the riots as an opportunity to illustrate his unpopularity as well as the diplomatic incompetence of the administration.[213] In contrast to the Rodríguez lynching, the Gomez lynching was not followed by demonstrations in Mexico, and the *San Antonio Light* believed that "the revolutionaries were not trying to take advantage of it."[214]

During the Rodríguez controversy, some people in Texas armed themselves to defend against a feared invasion from Mexico, while Mexicans living in the United States again appealed to the Mexican government for diplomatic action to demand that the United States deliver justice. President Díaz not only denounced the violence against Rodríguez, he imposed a boycott on imports from the United States and the Mexican government compensated the Rodríguez family. But no one was ever charged for the crime and Tejano leaders began looking for solutions other than diplomacy to solve the problem of violence.[215]

Even though the Thorndale event took place two hundred miles from Rock Springs, and even though the contexts were different, the abuse of civil rights connected the two events. The Rodríguez incident is significant because it set the stage for an even greater display of resentment in Texas when the Thorndale lynching took place eight months later. Mexicans in Texas knew that something needed to be done to prevent another failure of the Texas justice system to prosecute similar cases, and that the Mexican diplomats needed to act aggressively to prevent it from happening again.

As agents of the diplomatic arm of a foreign county, consuls sought to facilitate the flow of business between the foreign and the host countries. Another task was to assist and protect their citizens who were in the foreign land. Criticism of the consuls' ineffectiveness was present even before the Rodríguez lynching. In response to some prior complaints about segregation and discrimination in Texas schools, the diplomats, instead of probing the offending schools, supposedly conducted examinations of other selected schools and then sent a report to the national government minimizing the complaints. The Laredo newspaper editor, Nicasio Idar, criticized their meek response and cautioned his readers to expect the same results with any lynching cases such as the Rodríguez incident. The consuls, he wrote, instead of aggressively pursuing justice, would "excuse the criminals."[216]

Idar believed that the consuls were interested primarily in their own professional promotion and hoped to become higher ranking diplomats. By virtue of their class origins and education, they did not identify with the average Mexican in Texas. As a sympathizer of the revolutionaries Idar argued that the consuls were too closely allied with the Díaz regime and were actually spies for his government. The diplomats supposedly held the same views as the Díaz civil servants—the *científicos*—who aspired to modernize Mexico, but showed no enthusiasm in protecting the "interests of the homeland and the dignity of the nationals."[217]

The very nature of the consuls' tasks, however, required "diplomatic" solutions and therefore are easily criticized for insufficient vigor. And their tasks became even more complicated within the context of revolutionary Mexico. The Mexican diplomats needed to balance their public statements. On the one hand they needed to appease those Mexicans who called for a strong response to the Rodríguez and Gomez deaths and on the other to maintain the good relationship with the officials of the State of Texas. When the Thorndale lynching occurred, Miguel Diebold, the consul at San Antonio, sent Velardo to Thorndale to gather evidence, to identify Antonio's citizenship, and to transport the Gomez family to San Antonio for protection. Diebold then asked the governor for protection of the Mexican community, and at the same time he discouraged public demonstrations against the Colquitt administration.[218]

Shortly after the Rodríguez lynching, Madero, safe in San Antonio, drafted a proclamation calling for new elections and for armed resistance to Díaz. The date of Madero's action was November 20, 1910, and that date is generally considered the beginning of the Mexican Revolution. Even though Madero's group was small, other revolutionary leaders arose in opposition to Díaz, and military action began in May 1911 when Madero's allies captured Ciudad Juárez, near El Paso. Finally Díaz, by then eighty years old, resigned from his office at the end of May 1911 and sailed for Europe.

The interim president and the head of Mexico at the time of the Thorndale lynching was Francisco León de la Barra. De la Barra had held several diplomatic posts under Díaz thereby giving credence to Idar's claim that the consuls continued the Díaz policies. De la Barra disavowed any intention to seek office for himself and instead planned and supervised the new election.[219]

Madero won in the October election and became the head of the government in early November. Madero, however, was unable to control the nation and for the next ten years Mexico endured turmoil resulting in the death of as many as a million people. But it set the stage for the birth of modern Mexico and was a major factor in the creation of a concept of what it meant to be a Mexican. Not only did participants of the revolution spill over into Texas, but Mexicans living in Texas were drawn into the intellectual debate about their own identity.

The Mexican Revolution further weakened Mexico's attempts to pressure the United States concerning abuses of Mexican citizens in Texas and for the next ten years internal concerns took precedence. In the meantime, the turmoil generated within Mexico reached into Texas, especially along the border, an area where Madero was popular and where Mexican nationalism also germinated. In 1911 Governor Colquitt declared that Texas would not take sides in the factional disputes and instructed the Texas Rangers to enforce the law without favoring either side. The Rangers, who already were hated in the Mexican community, became even more unpopular because any actions, even those that were neutral, would give an advantage to one faction or another. The Mexican response to the Thorndale lynching, therefore, must be seen not only in the context of decades of resentment between Anglo and Mexican, but also in relation to the events in Mexico.[220]

Centers of Protest

One center of protest against the Thorndale lynching was Laredo, 150 miles southwest of San Antonio and on the Rio Grande. Laredo was significant because it was a major entry point between Mexico and Texas, and although it was not geographically in that part of Texas called "The Valley," Laredo was close enough to be associated with many of the region's discontents.

Laredo was also home to *La Crónica*, a newspaper that articulated some of those discontents and gave a voice to the Mexican population. The editor and owner of *La Crónica*, Nicasio Idar, was also involved in local politics, labor unions, and fraternal organizations. He began working in the printing business in the 1890s and eventually took over *La Crónica* which he produced with the assistance of three of his eight children. His career was cut short by his death in 1914, but his newspaper was influential under his brief leadership.[221]

It is important to note that neither the Thorndale nor the Rock Spring killings was the awakening event for Idar's criticism or for public protests by Mexicans. The public discontent over other conditions existed first and the two lynchings reinforced the belief that a stronger response was needed to resolve the problems. Although the issues that troubled the Mexicans and Tejanos along the Rio Grande were numerous and diverse, they can be grouped under three headings.

The first was the loss of the Tejano land base and the resultant weakening economic condition. This loss of land began in a minor way with the Treaty of Guadalupe Hidalgo, in 1848, which ended the Mexican War and added the land between the Nueces and Rio Grande to the state of Texas. In contrast to the conquest of Indian lands in other portions of the United States that resulted in "free" lands, the lands held by Mexico had been delineated and granted to Mexican citizens. Because the treaty did not guarantee the Mexicans their existing land grants, and because Texas had claimed the area between the two rivers, the United States authorized Texas to adjudicate the validity of land grants.

Texas established a special commission, and by 1852 most of the 234 claims had been adjudicated. Even given the circumstances and the conditions of the time, the work of the commission has been acknowledged as fair and honest. The change of government and the incorporation of the Spanish land titles into the Texas system, however, did set the stage and simplified the process for the sale of lands from Mexican owners to Anglo buyers, and from time to time some of the exchanges took place.[222]

In those years between the treaty and the arrival of railroads, the economic activity was largely ranching, and the social life of Anglos and Tejanos was relatively integrated. There were status differences in Mexican society between the *hacendados* (ranch owners), the *vaqueros* or cowboys, and the *peons* who worked on the ranches. There were also differences between the Anglo ranchers and merchants, but the various groups accommodated each other and there was even some intermarriage between Mexicans and Anglos.[223]

But the loss of land by the Texas Mexicans accelerated dramatically with the arrival of the railroads. Two railroads reached Laredo, the Texas Mexican Railroad from Corpus Christi in 1881, and the International & Great Northern from San Antonio in 1883. The railroads made commercial agriculture possible and ranches gave way to farms. The white population increased as settlers from the Midwest began migrating to the area. The population of Laredo grew from 3,521 in 1880 to 15,000 in 1911. Even some Wends from Thorndale migrated to Bishop, near Kingsville, in 1911. With financial resources the Anglos were able to make attractive offers and most of the land sales, just as the sale of the Liendo holdings in Milam County, were legal. On other occasions the sales, also legal, resulted from foreclosures and tax sales. And there were instances of illegal actions such as fraud and also intimidation. But the loss of land meant the loss of status.[224]

A second irritation was segregation, both in society and in schools. As the Anglo society grew in numbers Anglos separated themselves from the Mexican community and proceeded to transplant Anglo institutions into the region. Schools, for example, became segregated and the lessons were in English, not Spanish. And even in those schools that Mexican children attended, the English language and American culture were taught. The new Anglos did not understand the Spanish social classes and did not distinguish between the elite class and the laboring class. Mexicans were grouped, treated the same, and viewed as a source of cheap labor. Businesses such as barbershops, hotels, and restaurants also became segregated and Mexicans heard insults and derogatory names such as "greaser."[225]

The third discontent was over the failure of the Texas criminal justice system to enforce the law, especially in matters such as lynching and the protection of the rights of Mexican residents. The problem of law enforcement, especially along the border, was not new. For generations, rustlers had stolen livestock, cattle, horses, sheep, and goats and herded them across the international boundary. Further complicating the disorder, however, were the side-effects of the Mexican Revolution. Not only did Texas become a haven for refugees and a base for organizing an opposition, once the Revolution was underway Mexicans in Texas sided with opposing warring groups in Mexico.[226]

Local law enforcement was inadequate and the Texas State Rangers were sent the Rio Grande border to assist in maintaining the law and at the same time to remain neutral in the conflict between Mexican factions. Neither assignment made them popular. While the Rangers in the nineteenth century have been admired and romanticized by Anglos, some recent historians portrayed the Rangers of the twentieth century as oppressors. De León, for example, wrote that the Rangers were dedicated to keeping the Mexicans subservient. "In the 1910s, especially, they [the Rangers] carried out a campaign of execution against Tejanos of South Texas on the pretext that they were trying to put an end to Mexican revolutionary raids in the region."[227] And the Mexicans of the time were not enamored with the Rangers whom they called *los rinches*.[228]

Robert Utley finds it difficult to understand how a few Rangers could generate such great hostility. Although the 1901 act authorized four companies of eighty-nine men, the actual number in the entire force was much smaller. The size of the Ranger Force was dependent on the money appropriated by the legislature, and by 1911 the desire for low taxes and limited government brought down the number of Rangers to twenty-five. One company was stationed in Austin, another in Amarillo, and the third at San Benito in the Rio Grande Valley. The San Benito company was staffed by a captain and seven men and the distance from El Paso to Brownsville is 900 miles, giving weight to Utley's skepticism. Utley proposed an answer when he wrote that the term "*los rinches*" was used to identify not only Rangers, but any mounted white man with a gun. Rangers, after all, did not wear uniforms. The oppressive actions of sheriffs, deputies, federal customs inspectors, and cowboys, could have been assigned to the Rangers.[229]

While conceding the argument that scattered abuse toward Mexicans did indeed exist between 1880 and 1910, Utley maintains that intentional injustice by Rangers was rare. Most instances resulted from mistaken identity or misread circumstances—although few Mexicans could be convinced of that explanation.[230] And Montejano, quoting an attorney, Frank Pierce wrote: "Most of the killings, it was alleged, occurred while the officer would be attempting to make an arrest, the Mexican resisting and showing a disposition to injure."[231]

Within this context of multiple grievances, Idar, in January 1911, issued his call for a convention or *Congreso* to convene in Laredo. The proposal went out during the Díaz administration and two months after the Rodríguez lynching. Therefore, the congress was not in response to the Gomez death and most likely based on Idar's belief that no help was forthcoming from Díaz. The public response was positive and in March the decision was made to hold the convention in September to coincide with the holiday celebrating Mexican Independence. Gomez's death, in June, may have provided more immediacy for the plans and increased the attendance.

On September 14, 1911, approximately four hundred Texas-Mexican leaders met at Laredo for a week-long convention to discuss the problems in their communities and to search for solutions. The formal title was the *Congreso Mexicanista*. This is the congress José Limón referred to as a precursor of the 1960s Chicano movement.

The organizations that responded to Idar's call, and which Idar envisioned as the key to a solution, included the *Orden Caballeros de Honor* (Men's League of Honor), the Masonic Lodge, and numerous mutual aid societies that provided insurance, legal advice, or social opportunities. The *Orden Caballeros de Honor,* which Idar helped found, had chapters in approximately thirty Texas cities, and there were about twenty chapters of the Masonic Lodge in Mexican communities. In addition to the fraternal leaders there were journalists and Mexican diplomats in attendance.[232]

Idar, in his appraisal of the problem, ruled out both the Texas judicial system and the Mexican diplomats as solutions to the problems. Neither system had ended segregation in the schools or brought justice for the Rodríguez lynching. Instead Idar envisioned that the societies, temples, and clubs would rush to the aid of Mexicans in need. And if necessary the groups would collect money and take the case to Washington, the true center of power. "Mexican-Texans!" he wrote, "Let us unite and form a big and solid chain of fraternity. Let us each give our personal intellectual best and we will soon see our labors bear fruit." "Cortéz, Rodríguez, and Gómez ask for justice."[233]

Before the *Congreso* adjourned the delegates created two leagues, one for males, *La Grán Liga Mexicanista de Beneficencia y Protección,* one for females, *Liga Femenil Mexicanista.* The motto for both male and female leagues was *Por la Raza y Para la Raza*, and both leagues would confront the problems faced by Mexicans.[234] Even though the solutions proposed by the *Congreso* did not result in immediate results in racial harmony, it is historically significant in that it articulated some themes that became part of the Chicano movement in a later part of the century.[235]

The Thorndale lynching, which had preceded the congress by three months, had been thoroughly reported by *La Crónica,* and given the chronological proximity between the Thorndale lynching and the meeting of the congress, it is not difficult to assume that the Thorndale tragedy was the primary motivating factor for the meeting. The Thorndale lynching was not the catalyst for the congress, however, without doubt, it reinforced the views already ingrained in the Mexican mentality.

Part of the confusion of crediting the Thorndale lynching as the catalyst for the congress is tied to Carrigan and Webb, who in their article on lynching in the *Journal of Social History,* reversed the chronology of the lynching at Rock Springs and Thorndale. They described the Thorndale lynching first and wrote that it "appears to have provided the catalyst" for the Mexicans to organized themselves in defense of their civil rights.[236] Then they used the Rock Springs lynching as reason for Mexican protests and credit the diplomats with reducing the number of lynching cases.[237] In actuality, the diplomatic efforts following the Rock Springs lynching demonstrated to the Tejanos that the diplomats were not effective. There had to be another solution and that solution was through organizations of the citizens themselves.

For the people in Laredo, the driving force for the congress could better be described as a caldron rather than a catalyst. They met because of frustration with segregation, exploitation, and prejudice, rather than the Thorndale lynching. Idar wrote, "The bias against the Mexican is the evil that poisons the Texan-American organism. It destroys all good, it's the apple of discord in the Texas tree, the serpent that poisons the aspirations of every good American."[238] And by the time the congress met, the arrests in Thorndale had been made.

In contrast to Laredo's solution of using fraternal organizations for resolving the spectrum of discontents, a second center of protest, San

Antonio, focused its response specifically on the Thorndale lynching and directed its efforts toward the highest elected political officials of the state.

San Antonio was important because of the size of the Mexican population and its potential political power. Along with its more central geographical location and a long history of interaction with Anglos, Mexicans in San Antonio were more in the mainstream of Texas political life than the residents of Laredo. Instead of seeking relief through associations, the San Antonians' response specifically targeted the executive office of the state. The pressure on Governor Colquitt to intervene came from three sources in San Antonio, each with a distinct approach.

The first of the three sources was the newly appointed Mexican consul, Miguel E. Diebold. He had been inducted into the office on May 6, 1911, as a representative of the Díaz administration.[239] As a diplomat he needed to balance his actions bringing pressure to bear on the Texas officials to seek and punish the wrong-doers and to do so in a manner that was circumspect and respectful. And Diebold did that. He communicated with Governor Colquitt, he dispatched his representative, Velardo, to Cameron, and he employed a lawyer to follow the cases. He also informed his superiors in the Mexican Embassy of his activity. Diebold acted properly and should be credited with the prosecution being carried as far as it was.

The second source of pressure was from aforementioned Col. Francisco A. Chapa. As a political figure in San Antonio, he helped Colquitt get elected, and as a close friend and advisor, expressed his wishes in a quiet, personal manner. His appeal to Colquitt was valuable because Colquitt respected him as an ally and Chapa's communication was private and not inflammatory. Because of Chapa's sympathies for Díaz and his behind-the-scenes approach toward Colquitt, he was of a like mind with Diebold.

The third source of pressure on Colquitt came from the public in San Antonio and had the potential of damaging Colquitt's image if the demonstrations could not be controlled. The persons behind the protests were businessmen and merchants who held no official positions. With only self-restrain to limit the actions of these citizens, both Diebold and Colquitt were uneasy. An organization, formed on Sunday evening, June 25, 1911, six days after the Gomez lynching, was named the *Agrupacíon Protectura*

Mexicana or the Mexican Protective Association. The APM was entirely independent of the officials of Mexico, but promised to cooperate with the Mexican consuls when appropriate. The leaders included Donaciano R. Davila, a merchant who was elected president, and Emilio Flores, who became the secretary.[240]

Somewhat like Idar's *Congreso*, the APM cast a wider net than just the lynching of Gomez. Another form of abuse Mexicans experienced had surfaced in the neighboring community of New Braunfels. Instead of writing up legal contracts, Mexicans often made verbal agreements with land owners whereby they could clear land for farming and then continue as renters on the land they had cleared. In too many instances the landlords, after the land had been cleared, expelled the Mexicans and planted the crops themselves. While Diebold objected to the group's public opposition to lynching, he did not object to their program of mutual protection against landlord abuse.[241]

Diebold's fears of disruptive behavior were not realized and instead of calling for a public protest about lynching, the members of APM authorized their newly elected officers to send a telegram to Colquitt informing him that they would "anxiously await due compliance of the law" and that he would bring the criminals to justice. Colquitt responded the next day and informed them that he had already dispatched Assistant Attorney General Lane to Thorndale in response to a request from a citizen in Milam County. Colquitt also let them know that he preferred to use his administrative approach rather than to try the cases "under sensational newspaper reports."[242]

Another decision made at the opening meeting of APM was to hold a public gathering on the following Thursday in order to expand and formalize the organization. The officers scheduled the Hidalgo theater for the meeting and printed notices inviting the public. The notices, however, said nothing about Mexican renters in New Braunfels, and referred only to the Thorndale lynching. Diebold deplored the circular and hoped he could dissuade the participants from taking further action.[243]

CONVOCATORIA
AL PUEBLO
Mexicano y Mexico-Texano.

Por la presente se invita a los residentes de esta Ciudad a la

JUNTA GENERAL
que tendra lugar en el
SALON "HIDALGO"
ESQUINA DE LA CALLE DEL COMERCIO Y AVE. DE SANTA ROSA

EL JUEVES 29 DE JUNIO DE 1911
A LAS 8 EN PUNTO DE LA NOCHE.

PARA TRATAR DEL INFAME Y COBARDE
LINCHAMIENTO
COMETIDO EN THORNDALE, TEXAS, EN EL JOVEN MEXICANO DE 14 ANOS DE EDAD

Antonio Gomez.
"AGRUPACION PROTECTORA MEXICANA."

Presidente,
DONACIANO R. DAVILA.

Secretario,
EMILIO FLORES

SAN ANTONIO, TEXAS, JUNIO 27 DE 1911

IMPRENTA 415 Zavala St. MENDOZA PRINTING CO

Davila's Broadside.
The notice called for a meeting to protest
the lynching of Antonio Gomez.
Courtesy Archivo Histórico Genero Estrada

More than 3,000 people attended the event and it was described in the *San Antonio Light* as "one of the most enthusiastic, yet orderly, assemblages of Mexicans that the city has ever witnessed." The group agreed to confront the legal problems by setting up branches in every Mexican community in Texas, with the headquarters in San Antonio to coordinate the program, and to stage a mass meeting in San Antonio to protest the lynching of Mexicans.[244]

Davila and Flores then sent a second telegram, this time to Attorney General Lane as he went to Cameron to oppose the granting of bail to any of the defendants. Their message was basically the same as in their telegram to Colquitt: they expected Lane to do his duty. Lane expressed his displeasure to M. A. Esteva, a Mexican diplomat in San Antonio, and informed him that Texas public servants would perform their duty without any threat of being watched. He considered the Mexicans who were raising a public clamor to be misguided, misled, and over-zealous and asked Esteva if something could be done to stop their unjust criticism of the governor and the public officials. Lane even hinted that persistent pressure could build resentment in American citizens who were potential jurors and jeopardize the prosecution of the case.[245]

Although both the Laredo and the San Antonio protests were helpful in raising awareness of the Thorndale lynching, the San Antonio appeals were more important in influencing Governor Colquitt. Not only did Colquitt ask for a court of inquiry, but he also instructed the assistant attorney general to help the county prosecutors with the trials. However, once the jury went into its chambers for deliberations, the power of executive office stopped at the door.

Mexican Perceptions and Misperceptions of the Lynching

News of the Thorndale lynching reached the pages of both the *Austin Statesman* and the *San Antonio Express* the next day, June 20, and Laredo's *La Crónica* on June 29. The early details were sketchy and inaccurate, leading the Mexican readers to interpret what they read through their own personal experience in Texas. In the same sense that the neural pathways were manicured by the past for the residents of Thorndale, so also were those of the Mexicans. Perception was important, and the lynching was just another piece of evidence that supported their image of reality.

Mexicans correctly understood the Texas judicial system and they realized that the decision of guilt was made by a jury and not the president or governor. They doubted that the lynch mob would be punished. They believed that the accused would be released on bail, make two or three appearances in court, and after public interest subsided, the case would be closed. As Idar stated, "We do not remember that any American has been punished for lynching a Mexican, even though some have done it."[246]

The Mexicans, also correctly, did not view the murder of Zieschang as murder in the first degree because it was not premeditated. Gomez did not plan the murder or lie in wait for Zieschang, and the events that led to the stabbing were accidental. The homicide, therefore, would not be punished with death or life imprisonment. Yet the men who lynched Gomez made him pay with his life.[247]

The Mexicans incorrectly assumed, however, that Gomez was lynched by "a band of Germans" because reports had identified Zieschang as a German. Understandably they did not know Zieschang was a Wend, and by then the Wends had entered the German culture. However, their assumption was that everyone in town was a German and that only Germans were involved in the lynching. And one account claimed that the members of the mob filed past the suspended Gomez, shook his hand and asked him "if he wanted to kill more Germans."[248]

So while journalists such as Idar condemned the actions of the Germans and proposed a boycott of German businesses, they justified Gomez's action as a Mexican. They first defended him by referencing their own code of honor and saying that he had been insulted and that Zieschang humiliated him when he took the shingle from him. Some reports placed the stabbing into the context of a fight thereby justifying the stabbing, and Idar tried to make the stabbing look accidental: "The boy had the pocket knife in his hand, and when he stood up, perhaps in an involuntary movement, trying to avoid a blow from the German, he cut him above the heart."[249]

Instead of identifying the preliminary stage of the Zieschang murder as a controversy over littering, Mexicans saw the context as segregation. *La Crónica* reported that Gomez had been asked to leave a place of business and when he refused, a fight ensued. To Mexicans living in the Rio Grande Valley, segregation as the underlying cause made sense to them. And the Rio Grande Valley perspective is further demonstrated when the Mexican press blamed the lynching on the Rangers—*los rinches*. Prior to the lynching there were no Rangers in Thorndale. However, if the definition of "*los rinches*" is broadened to include any armed white man, then the accusation is understandable.

Journalists also filled the information gaps by adding details from previous lynching cases. The Rodríguez lynching may have been the inspiration for some accounts that stated that Gomez was taken out of the jail and lynched while he was awaiting trial. And with reports from many Southern lynchings fresh in their minds, they embellished the narrative by stating that the mob, after hanging Gomez, dragged his body around town behind a buggy.

Even though the telling of the Gomez lynching may fall short in the details, one should not conclude that the incident and the protests that followed were not significant in the future struggle for civil rights. They were. In 2002, in a session in which a textbook publisher solicited criticisms of a school text, a reviewer, Mrs. Lupita Ramirez commented that more information should be included about the Mexican civil rights struggle. And as evidence she stated: "In June 1911, a white mob in Thorndale, Texas put 14-year old Antonio Gomez to death and his body was dragged around town tied to the back of a buggy. He was accused of killing a German Texan in a fight after refusing to leave a place of business." Even though her recommendation to expand the topic may have been valid, her evidence was flawed.[250]

Most likely scholars researching conditions of Mexicans in Texas worked out of the pages of *La Crónica* and assumed the accuracy of the news stories because the narrative matched their assumptions. The inaccurate elements in the reports should not be ignored because they provide insights into the Mexican community's view of things in the early part of the century. However, contemporary scholarship must refine the historical narrative and expand the perspective in order to draw a more complete portrait of Mexicans in Texas.[251]

VII. AFTERMATH

The Decline of Lynching

There is no debate over the fact that lynching deaths declined early in the twentieth century, in both Texas and the nation. That trend line of diminishing numbers was evident before the Thorndale lynching and it continued downward after 1911. The last Mexican lynched in the United States was Rafael Benavides in Farmington, New Mexico on November 16, 1928. The lynching of blacks lasted longer, and not until 1936 did the number of such deaths annually reach single digit numbers, and the widely publicized lynching of Emmett Till took place as late as 1955.[252]

Scholars, however, have not agreed on a specific cause of the decline. One contributing element could have been anti-lynching legislation passed by several states. Some states, including Texas, approved such legislation before the end of the nineteenth century, although these laws were meaningless unless they were enforced. The United States Congress considered passing legislation on several occasions, but anti-lynching bills were repeatedly blocked in the Senate. There was no federal law prohibiting lynching until Lyndon Johnson's term of office when Congress included it the Civil Rights Act of 1968.[253]

More credit has been given to anti-lynching efforts carried on by newspapers, individuals, and organizations. Newspapers began to describe the inhumane elements of a lynching and the *Chicago Tribune*, as early as 1882, began nationwide tracking of incidents. The *New York Times* reported the Thorndale lynching and other newspapers reprinted the story. Institutions and organizations such as the Tuskegee Institute collected and dispersed information on lynching, and the National Association for the Advancement of Colored People launched its anti-lynching campaign in 1910 the year after its founding. And there were individuals who contributed by keeping these acts in the limelight and illustrating their brutality. Ida B. Wells, a teacher and journalist in Memphis, began her crusade in 1892; and Jessie Daniel Ames of Georgetown, Texas founded the Association of Southern Women for the Prevention of Lynching in 1930 and became its president.[254]

In recent years critics of capital punishment have argued that lynching declined because it was replaced by the more socially acceptable procedure of capital punishment. The goals and results of state executions were the same as lynching, so lynching was no longer necessary. Even though state executions, they insist, no longer resembled the traditional lynching spectacles, they are still "legal lynchings."[255]

The dominant element that helped formulate criticism of the Thorndale lynching fits most closely with the role of public opinion. By the time of the Thorndale lynching attitudes had already begun to change and condemnation of all lynching was widespread.

The public conversation over the Thorndale lynching illustrates that such a stigma against lynching had already been formed before 1911 and without it there probably would have been no arrests and trials. Newspaper headlines used words such as "Deplorable," "tragedy," and "regrettable." The editor of the *Rockdale Reporter and Messenger* wrote, "It is the duty of every newspaper, in the interest of good government, to denounce mob violence wherever found under the guise of punishment for crime." The lynching "has brought the fair name of Milam County and all Texas down to disgrace." "[Mob] violence is a crime against the government and should be discountenanced in all its forms by every law-abiding citizen of this great commonwealth." "No matter the circumstances leading up to this affair, Milam County must bow her head in shame over the horrible occurrence in our sister city Monday night...." "The spirit of mob violence must be curbed, and the Thorndale disgrace should be thoroughly sifted."[256] Image was important and when the *San Antonio Express* reported that the best citizens of Thorndale participated in the lynching the *Thorndale Thorn's* editor came to the town's defense. E. L. Ramsey called the reports sent to the daily papers misleading and their comments unjust. "We think these papers should have withheld their comments until they could have become fully acquainted with the facts and better acquainted with the citizenship of Thorndale." Although the population was only about 1,000, the portion of "fair minded and law abiding people" was as high as in Galveston, Houston and any other places in Texas. "The noble people of Thorndale regret the occurrence very much."[257] The lesson, nevertheless, was unmistakable; to avoid being portrayed in a negative way, avoid lynching.

And Judge Ed English, also responding to the San Antonio newspaper's accusations, on June 24, gave a statement to the press in an attempt to correct some "erroneous statements which tend to reflect upon Milam county and her citizens." In it he summarized the major points of the incident and then defended the "best citizens of Thorndale" because they "testified freely as to all the facts" and they commended the governor for "offering his assistance to suppress mob violence if necessary." Then he singled out the statement of the Thorndale correspondent for the San Antonio newspaper and said that it was "wide of the mark."[258] Yet he failed to say which part of society was responsible.

So, while the response to Thorndale's lynching was in part the result of public disapproval, the prosecution of the cases, may in turn, have provided an important stimulus for accelerating the decline of lynching. The prosecution pattern in place at that time, even though the stigma had been linked to lynching, was a ritual of non-enforcement. However, following the Thorndale lynching four men, guilty or not, were indicted and three were actually tried. The law was enforced the way the laws were written. There was a court of inquiry, a grand jury, bail hearings, the careful selection of juries, testifying of witnesses, cross examination, change of venue, and observers from the Mexican government. Assigning criminal liability to suspects and painstakingly working through the legal process was instructive to anyone who was watching, and may well have been a factor in the further decline of lynching.[259]

Families of the Victims and the Lives of the Accused

Karl Zieschang, Jr., was remembered on Wednesday afternoon, June 21st, at St. Paul's church and buried in the congregation's cemetery. The attendance at the funeral service was so large that, even after seating the children on the steps leading to the altar, all the people could not find a place inside the church building.[260] A modest granite tombstone marks his grave in the congregation's cemetery and on it is inscribed:

Christus ist mein Leben,

Sterben is mein Gewinn

Dem thu ich mich ergeben

Mit Freud fahr ich dahin.

[Christ is my life, Dying is my victory, I yield myself to him, With joy do I depart.]

The widow, Annie, who was twenty-five-years old at the time of the murder, later married Richard Kieschnick, a widowed farmer in Williamson County and then gave birth to three more children. She lived until 1975.

Karl Zieschang's tombstone.

Antonio Gomez's burial went unheralded. Constable McCoy removed Antonio's body from the ladder and took it to the owner of a Mexican store in Thorndale hoping to leave the body there. The owner declined and it was most likely McCoy who took the body to the Gamez home in Williamson County. Albert Moerbe, Gamez's employer, was also the younger brother of the widowed Mrs. Zieschang. He permitted Gabriel to bury his son on the property, but informed Gabriel that he was no longer welcome and instructed him that he and his family were to leave the property by 5:00 P.M. that day. Gamez believed that his life was in danger, so after a hurried burial he entrusted some of his possessions to a neighbor and took only some bedding as the family made its way to the railroad station in Taylor—by 6:00 P.M. With the assistance of Vice Counsul Velardo, the family traveled to San Antonio. There, on June 22, Gabriel dictated a statement giving his knowledge of the event.[261] On June 26 he returned to Williamson County to retrieve his possessions. His train fare was provided by the *Agrupacíon* in San Antonio.[262]

Gabriel died eleven years later on October 26, 1922, at Elgin, near Austin. The following year the United States and Mexico signed an agreement that set up machinery for arbitrating damage claims filed in the two respective countries. Two of Gabriel's daughters, Dolores, who had married Indalicio Gonzalez and was living in Galveston, and Maria, who had married Lauro Rodriguez and was living in Austin, initiated a case for damages resulting from the death of their brother, Antonio. The United States contested the claims, largely because the crime had taken place prior to the diplomatic agreement.[263]

After the trial, Z. T. Gore, Jr. remained in Milam County and took up farming. In 1917 he registered for the draft and in1918 he enlisted. He served for nine months and was stationed at El Paso when his unit was demobilized. His next residence was in Wichita Falls, the scene of an oil boom. The first producing field in Wichita County had been at Electra in 1911 and a pipeline took the crude oil to Dallas and Fort Worth for refining. By 1915 Wichita County had 1,025 producing wells and by 1920 there were nine refineries in the county. Gore worked as a cook in a café and lived in the Seventh Street Rooming House. He was unmarried. From time to time he traveled to Ft Leavenworth, Kansas for medical care and was a resident in the old soldiers' home when he died on May 27, 1958.[264]

Garrett Noack also left Thorndale to work in the new petroleum industry, but in the southeastern part of the state. In 1918 he was working as a foreman for the Texas Company in Port Arthur. Two years later, however, he had moved to Liberty County, west of Port Arthur where he rented a farm on the Cleveland to Dayton Road. His family continued to grow until there were eight children. He died at Dayton on December 23, 1960.[265]

Ezra Stephens had married Nancy Myrle Locklin (called Myrle) within days after his trial. In 1915 he became a father and gave the son his name. At the time he registered for the draft, in 1917, he identified himself as an unemployed mechanic. That same year, he enlisted and served in the Student Army Training Corps of the University of Texas, stationed at Camp Mabry. In 1920, having separated from his wife, he lived with his widowed mother who kept a boarding house in Thorndale. Ezra was the electrician at the power house.

By 1930 he had been reunited with his wife and together with his mother, a second son, four years of age, and an adopted daughter moved to Corpus Christi. He worked as an auto salesman and Myrle was a salesperson in a dry goods store. They did own a radio, but the house was a rented one. He died on December 12, 1933, of lung cancer, and was buried in Thorndale.[266]

Harry Wuensche's life was devastated by epilepsy. Just when he suffered his first seizure is not known. Nothing indicates any epilepsy prior to the 1911 lynching and he lived an active life. In 1909, for example, he had traveled to the San Antonio Fair and in 1911 he and his father-in-law went to Austin to hear a speech by Eugene Debs, Socialist candidate for the presidency of the United States.[267]

After their first child, which had been born December 18, 1910, prior to the lynching, Harry became the father of a son on May 19, 1912, and another daughter on November 11, 1913. All three were born in Thorndale

However, in 1920 he was a resident in the Texas State Epileptic Colony in Abilene. The state-owned institution had opened its doors in March 1904 and by August it was filled to capacity with 201 patients. A colony such as this was necessary because at that time effective treatments or medications were not available. Controlling seizures through managing the daily life of the patients was the accepted practice at the institution, although the medical staff experimented with injections of rattlesnake venom as a better method of treatment. Harry worked on the property as a gardener and from time to time returned to Milam County for a visit. He died in 1922 and was buried north of Thorndale in the Detmold cemetery.[268] His mother remained his closest support during his difficult years and was later buried in a grave next to his.

Other Participants

Although prohibition had been the principle issue in Governor Colquitt's first election, it was the Mexican Revolution, which lasted from 1910 to 1920, that commanded his attention throughout his two terms. The political alliance and the friendship between Colquitt and Chapa that began with prohibition continued during the revolutionary decade as well. Chapa's newspaper, *El Imparcial de Texas*, had supported the Díaz regime, and after Díaz's departure for Europe, Chapa transferred his loyalty to General Bernardo Reyes who tried to take power after Díaz. Chapa was an important ally for Reyes because of his ties to Colquitt, the person who issued orders to the Rangers on the Rio Grande. The three did meet in Austin on October 16, 1911, to discuss ways of avoiding Ranger interference with Reyes.[269] Federal authorities, however, intervened and as a result of Chapa's association with Reyes and for assisting him in the purchase of arms and raising a military force in Texas, Chapa was found guilty of violating federal neutrality laws. Colquitt quickly persuaded President William Howard Taft to grant Chapa a pardon.

And then in 1913 Chapa persuaded Colquitt to pardon Gregorio Cortez Lira. Cortez had been sentenced to life imprisonment for the killing of a sheriff, but many Tejanos believed the killing was justified and Cortez became a symbol of resistance to the heavy-handed Anglos. Cortez also became the hero in a *corrido* (ballad) and more recently became even more famous as a result of Américo Paredes' book entitled *With His Pistol in His Hand*.[270] When Chapa died in 1924 Colquitt was one of the honorary pall bearers.[271]

Miguel Diebold was removed from his position as consul in San Antonio by the Madero administration. No reason was given. His previous loyalty to Díaz may have been a consideration, or his statement given in a newspaper interview that Texas was hell for Mexicans may have been the reason. Diebold insisted that he had been misquoted.[272]

Constable Robert L. McCoy, still single, moved to Houston to work at the Midland Ship Yard; and Wilford Wilson moved to Thrall to manage a lumberyard.[273]

Thorndale after the Lynching

For much of the country, 1900 may have been the date for entering the modern century, but for Thorndale the pivotal date could well have been 1911. Symbolically, the lynching was an act befitting the previous century while the arrests and trials, even though there were no convictions, symbolized the beginning of the modern age. And for Thorndale the decade that followed the lynching was a period of growth and modernization.

One of the most noticeable modern developments came in that decade when Thorndale became involved with another kind of oil: rock oil. Drillers struck petroleum deposits west of Thorndale, near Thrall, in 1915 and drilled 200 wells. In 1920 Thorndale was home to ten men who worked with petroleum. Their occupations ranged from geologist to driller. The petroleum industry's first product had been kerosene for illumination, and by the end of the nineteenth century it also supplied oil as a fuel for steam engines and home furnaces. Thorndale's brush with petroleum came with the development of the internal combustion engine and its reliance on gasoline. In Texas the gusher at Spindletop on January 10, 1901 ushered in the new era and an oil boom followed. Cotton continued as the single major economic activity in Texas, but oil grew to a close second. In 1896 Texas had produced 1,000 barrels of oil and in 1902 it had produced 21,000,000.[274]

As Thorndale grew, it built on its pre-1911 accomplishments. In 1920, the city water system, which had taken so long to resolve, employed one person to manage the water works. The cottonseed oil mill in 1920 had expanded and employed thirty-four men. Seventeen men worked with automobiles. The telephone nudged the telegraph aside. Only one person was employed by Western Union telegraph, but three worked with the telephone. Three citizens were typists. There was even an entertainment industry with one person managing the picture show. And there were four persons, most likely a traveling troupe, who identified themselves as actors and actresses of the theater and stage living in Thorndale. Construction had slowed but ten men were carpenters and painters and four worked in the lumber industry. Stock keeping, which employed four men, gave way to cotton which directly provided jobs for eleven men and indirectly for thirteen who worked for the dray lines.[275]

One final difference between 1911 and 1920 was the absence of Thorndale's signature saloons. The prohibitionists, after losing the battles on the state level finally won the war, and nation-wide Prohibition began in 1919. And in Thorndale, as in the nation, production of alcoholic beverages shifted to sheds and cellars and became a cottage industry. The owners of empty saloon buildings needed to find other tenants and the Old Bank Saloon once more became a bank. The census of 1920 listed no bartenders or bar owners.[276]

Thorndale finally became incorporated as a town in 1923. Two years later it quietly achieved recognition of its urban status from the Sanborn Fire Insurance Map Company.[277] Beginning in 1867 this company mapped all the major cities and towns in the country block by block and building by building. The surveyors and analysts drew large-scale maps showing the buildings, their use, construction materials, available water and fire services—all kinds of information insurance companies would need to set insurance fees. Although the map of Thorndale was drawn fourteen years after the lynching, the basic design of the town and locations of buildings were much the same in 1925 as they had been in 1911. And not much changed after that. In recent years some of the buildings have crumbled and most have different tenants, but the map still remains true and ties together the present town with the town that was the stage for a century-old tragedy.

Notes

PREFACE

1   José E. Limón, "El Primer Congreso Mexicanista de 1911: A Precursor to Contemporary Chicanismo," *Aztlán* (1974): 85–117.

2   William D. Carrigan and Clive Webb, "The Lynching of Persons of Mexican Origin or Descent in the United States, 1848 to 1928," *Journal of Social History* (Winter 2003): 417.

3   My argument follows a similar line of reasoning as that of Richard Maxwell Brown in *Strain of Violence: Historical Studies of American Violence and Vigilantism* (New York: Oxford University Press, 1975). In it he details the presence of violence in the United States from the colonial era to contemporary times and argues that the violence of the 1960s built on the preceding violence. The violence in central Texas, for example, influenced President Lyndon Johnson and his pursuit of the conflict in Vietnam.

4   Thorndale's population in 2009 was 1,309.

CHAPTER I. THE MURDER AND LYNCHING

5   Acervo Histórico Diplomático, NC4110-4, 16-4-27, Archivo Histórico Genero Estrada, Secretaría de Relaciones Exteriores, Mexico City. The copy of the testimonies survived largely because Consul Miguel E. Diebold requested a copy from Governor Oscar B. Colquitt. The copy was eventually deposited in the diplomatic archives in Mexico City.

CHAPTER II. EUROPEAN SETTLEMENT OF MILAM AND WILLIAMSON COUNTIES

6   Donald E. Chipman, *Spanish Texas 1519–1821* (Austin: University of Texas Press, 1992), 150–153, 156.

7   Lelia M. Batte, *History of Milam County, Texas* (San Antonio: The Naylor Company, 1956), 10, 11; Herbert E. Bolton, *Texas in the Middle Eighteenth Century* (Austin: University of Texas Press, 1970), 159, 185, 231; *Thorndale Thorn*, March 22, 1907; Kathleen K. Gilmore, *The San Xavier*

Missions: A Study in Historical Site Identification (Austin: State Building Commissions Report 16, 1969).

8   Chipman, 156; Bolton, 159, 231; Odie B. Faulk, *The Last Years of Spanish Texas 1778–1821* (The Hague: Mouton & Co., 1964), 83.

9   Thomas Fleming, *The Louisiana Purchase* (Hoboken, N.J., John Wiley and Sons, 2003), 127.

10   Charles W. Hackett, *Pichardo's Treatise on the Limits of Louisiana and Texas* (Austin: University of Texas Press, 1934), 2: 106, 343.

11   Clara Sterns Scarbrough, *Land of Good Water: A Williamson County, Texas, History* (Georgetown, TX: Williamson County Sun Publishers, 1973), 75.

12   Batte, 35, 47, 49.

13   Scarbrough, 121.

14   Noah Smithwick, *Evolution of a State or Recollections of Old Texas Days* (Austin: W. Thomas Taylor, 1995), 168, 183; Faulk, 83; J. Frank Dobie, *The Longhorns* (New York: Bramhall House, 1982), 18.

15   Batte, 55.

16   Batte, 55, 56; *Handbook of Texas Online*, s.v. "Milam County," http://www.tshaonline.org/handbook/online/articles/MM/hcm13.html   (accessed September 3, 2007).

17   William B. Bizzell, *Rural Texas* (New York: The Macmillan Company, 1924), 4.

18   Scarbrough, 3.

19   Scarbrough, 141.

20   Harry E. Chrisman, *The Ladder of Rivers: The Story of I. P. (Print) Olive* (Athens, OH: Swallow Press Books, 1962), 28, 31.

21   J. Frank Dobie, *A Vaquero in the Brush Country* (New York: Grosset & Dunlap, 1929), 22–29.

22   *Handbook of Texas Online*, s.v. "Hide and Tallow Trade," http://www.tshaonline.org/handbook/online/articles/HH/dfh1.html   (accessed September 3, 2007).

23 Chrisman, 28–29.

24 Chrisman, 87–89, 93.

25 Carl H. Moneyhon, *Texas after the Civil War: The Struggle of Reconstruction* (College Station: Texas A & M University Press, 2004), 48, 101; S. G. Reed, *A History of the Texas Railroads* (Houston: The St. Clair Publishing Co., 1941), 314.

26 Moneyhon, 152.

27 Reed, 314–315; *Handbook of Texas Online*, s.v. "Houston and Great Northern Railroad," http://www.tshaonline.org/handbook/online/articles/HH/eqh8.html (accessed August 30, 2007).

28 Donald R. Walker, *Penology for Profit: A History of the Texas Prison System, 1867–1912* (College Station: Texas A & M University Press, 1988), 31, 32.

29 Walker, 34, 43.

30 Reed, 318; Moneyhon, 151; W. C. Nunn, *Texas under the Carpetbaggers* (Austin: University of Texas Press, 1962), 34, 35.

31 *Handbook of Texas Online*, s.v. "International-Great Northern Railroad," http://www.tshaonline.org/handbook/online/articles/II/eqi4.html (accessed August 30, 2007); Reed, 319.

32 Deed from Solidad Liendo to International and Great Northern Railroad, February 8, 1877, March 29, 1877, vol. D1, p. 174, Clerk of Milam County, Cameron, Texas. Another purchase was from C. H. Williams on May 3, 1875.

33 Moneyhon, 191, 203. The amendment to permit land grants was passed in 1873.

34 Thomas Lloyd Miller, *The Public Lands of Texas 1519–1970* (Norman: University of Oklahoma Press, 1972), 102; *Handbook of Texas Online*, s.v. "International-Great Northern Railroad;" "New York and Texas Land Company," http://www.tshaonline.org/handbook/online/articles/NN/ufn2.html. (accessed August 30, 2007).

35 Scarbrough, 302.

36 Texas Transportation Archives://www. ttarchives.com/Library/Index (accessed September 3, 2007).

37   The railroad reached its goal, Laredo, in December 1881. *Handbook of Texas Online*, s.v. "International-Great Northern Railroad."

38   Scarbrough, 199.

39   *Handbook of Texas Online*, s.v. "Milam County."

40   John S. Spratt, *The Road to Spindletop: Economic Change in Texas 1875–1901* (Dallas: Southern Methodist University Press, 1955), 278.

41   *Handbook of Texas Online*, s.v. "Milam County."

42   *Handbook of Texas Online*, s.v. "Williamson County," http://tshaonline.org/handbook/online/articles/WW/hcw11.html   (accessed September 5, 2007).

43   *Handbook of Texas Online*, s.v. "Milam County."

44   University of Virginia, Geospatial and Statistical Data Center: http://fisher.lib.virginia.edu/collections/stats/histcensus/index.html (accessed November 12, 2009). Total farms: 5055.

45   The white population also declined early in the century, but at a lesser rate than the decline of the black population.

46   1900 U. S. Census, population schedule, Milam County, Texas, Precinct 8, Enumeration District No. 82, sheets 8–10. Ancestry.com://www.ancestry.com (accessed January 10, 2007); 1910 U. S. Census, population schedule, Milam County, Texas, Precinct 8, Enumeration District No. 72, sheets 1–10. Ancestry.com://www.ancestry.com (accessed January 15, 2007).

47   Gerald Stone, *The Smallest Slavonic Nation: The Sorbs of Lusatia* (London: The Athlone Press, 1972), 3–4, 8–15. Their only hope for gaining nationhood came after the German defeat in World War I. In keeping with Woodrow Wilson's concept of self-determination of nations, the Wends petitioned the Allies meeting at the Versailles conference to grant them nationhood. Even though Poland and Czechoslovakia became nations, the Wends' request was ignored and they continued their minority status within Germany.

48   George R. Nielsen, *In Search of a Home: Nineteenth-Century Wendish Immigration* (College Station: Texas A & M University Press, 1989), 53.

49   George C. Engerrand, *The So-called Wends of Germany and Their Colonies in Texas and in Australia,* Study, no. 7, University of Texas Bulletin no. 3417 (Austin: [University of Texas] Bureau of Research in the Social

Sciences, 1934), 124; Deed from Benj. R. Townsend and J. A. Chandler to Peter Zieschang, September 22, 1871, vol. 13, p.291, Clerk of Williamson County, Georgetown, Texas.

50   Terry G. Jordan, John L. Bean, and William M. Holmes, *Texas: A Geography* (Boulder: Westview Press, 1984), 201, 202.

51   Brand Book, County Clerk, Williamson County, No. 53, p, 272; Scarbrough, 293; Chrisman, 133, 180.

52   Criminal Minutes, 1ˢᵗ Dist. Court, Vol. 1, p. 289, 294, Williamson County, Georgetown, Texas.

53   Joseph Wilson, ed., trans., *Baptismal Records of St. Paul Lutheran Church, Serbin, Texas 1854–1883* (Easley, SC: Southern Historical Press, 1985), 259, 260. In 1890 the Lutherans at Noack established their own congregation.

54   Deed from P. W. Johnson to Andrew Polnick, January 8, 1880, Book 30, p. 23, Clerk of Williamson County, Georgetown, Texas; George R. Nielsen, "The Wends at Thorndale and Noack," *Newsletter of the Texas Wendish Heritage Society* (April 2008): 10–12.

55   Deed from W. G. Carothers to Charles Michalk, June 5, 1884, Book 13, p. 385, Clerk of Milam County, Cameron, Texas.

56   B. B. Paddock, ed., *A History of Central and Western Texas* (Chicago: The Lewis Publishing Co., 1911), 2: 611, 615.

57   University of Virginia, Geospatial and Statistical Data Center.

58   1910 U. S. Census, population schedule, Milam County, Texas, Precincts 1–8. Ancestry.com://www.ancestry.com (accessed November 20, 2009); *Handbook of Texas Online*, s.v. "Rockdale, Texas," http://www.tshaonline.org/handbook/online/articles/RR/hfr8.html (accessed December 5, 2009); Roberto R. Calderón, *Mexican Coal Mining Labor in Texas and Coahuila 1880–1930* (College Station: Texas A & M University Press, 2000), 168, 169. Calderón states that there were between 1,500 and 2,000 Mexicans in Milam County in the early 1900s, double the numbers on the 1910 census lists.

59   1910 U. S. Census, population schedule, Caldwell County, Texas, Precinct 5, Enumeration District 33, sheet 14, dwelling 165, family 268, Gabriel Gomez household. Ancestry.com://www.ancestry.com, (accessed January 20, 2007). Acervo Histórico Diplomático, NC4110-4, 16-4-27,

Archivo Histórico Genero Estrada, Secretaría de Relaciones Exteriores, Mexico City.

60   University of Virginia, Geospatial and Statistical Data Center.

CHAPTER III.   THORNDALE'S GROWTH AND BOOMER MENTALITY

61   Deed from Soledad Liendo to W. S. Carothers, January 12, 1878, vol. D2, p. 515, Clerk of Milam County, Cameron, Texas.

62   Clara Stearns Scarbrough, *Land of Good Water: A Williamson County, Texas, History* (Georgetown, Texas: Williamson County Sun Publishers, 1973), 458; [Milam County Heritage Preservation Society], *Matchless Milam: History of Milam County Texas* (Dallas: Taylor Publishing Co., 1984), 35.

63   Lelia M. Batte, *History of Milam County, Texas* (San Antonio: The Naylor Company, 1956), 174.

64   *Matchless Milam,* 35; Scarbrough, 458.

65   1880 U. S. Census, population schedule, Milam County, Texas, Precinct 5, Enumeration District 105, sheets 49–51. Ancestry.com://www. ancestry.com (accessed January 28, 2006).

66   Deed from W. S. Carothers to International & Great Northern Railroad, March 15, 1881, vol. 8, p. 402, Clerk of Milam County, Cameron, Texas.

67   *Thorndale Thorn,* June 27, 1902.

68   *Thorndale Thorn,* February 14, 1902; February 20, 1903; April 1, 1904; February 14, 1902. The population was 700 in 1902.

69   *Thorndale Thorn,* January 22, 1909; July 9, 1904.

70   1900 U. S. Census, population schedule, Milam County, Texas, Precinct 8, Enumeration District No. 82, sheets 8–10. Ancestry.com://www. ancestry.com (accessioned January 10, 2007); *Thorndale Thorn,* February 14, 1902.

71   *Thorndale Thorn,* March 31, 1911; October 8, 1909.

72   1910 U. S. Census, population schedule, Milam County, Texas, Precinct 8, Enumeration District No. 72, sheets 1–10. Ancestry.com://www. ancestry.com (accessed January 15, 2007).

73   *Thorndale Thorn*, February 26, 1909.

74   *Thorndale Thorn*, March 5, 1909; April 23, 1909.

75   *Thorndale Thorn*, August 20, 1909.

76   *Thorndale Thorn*, November 5, 1909; November 26, 1909.

77   Deed Records, vol. 107, p. 349; vol. 179, p. 603–4, Clerk of Milam County, Cameron, Texas. Thorndale was incorporated in 1923. Batte, 174.

78   *Thorndale Thorn*, July 29, 1904.

79   *Thorndale Thorn*, June 14, 1907.

80   *Thorndale Thorn*, April 14, 1911; January 8, 1909; January 22, 1909; February 19, 1909.

81   *Thorndale Thorn*, April 22, 1910.

82   *Thorndale Thorn*, July 9, 1904; February 15, 1907; January 22, 1909; February 12, 1909. The 1920 Census provides evidence for the vitality of the Opera House. It listed two young couples who identified themselves as actors and actresses. 1920 U. S. Census, population schedule, Milam County, Texas, Precinct 8, Enumeration District 137, sheet 7, dwelling 133, family 135 and 136. Ancestry.com://www.ancestry.com (accessed January 17, 2007).

83   *Thorndale Thorn*, February 23, 1906; May 7, 1909; April 9, 1909.

84   S. G. Reed, *A History of the Texas Railroads* (Houston: The St. Clair Publishing Co., 1941), 738, 739; *Texas Almanac and State Industrial Guide for 1911* (Galveston: A. H. Belo & Company, 1911), 182; William B. Bizzell, *Rural Texas* (New York: The Macmillan Company, 1924), 266.

85   *Thorndale Thorn*, March 20, 1903; November 5, 1909, March 18, 1910; November 25, 1910. The land was purchased from Charles Moerbe.

86   *Thorndale Thorn*, June 5, 1903; *Texas Almanac 1911*, 120-127.

87   *Thorndale Thorn*, February 12, 1909; March 18, 1910.

88   *Thorndale Thorn*, February 24, 1911; May 5, 1911.

89   *Texas Almanac*, 1911, 127.

90   *Texas Almanac*, 1911, 127; *Thorndale Thorn*, November 26, 1909.

91   Scarbrough, 349.

92   *Thorndale Thorn*, August 27, 1909.

93   *Thorndale Thorn*, January 28, 1910; March 4, 1910; March 25, 1910.

94   *Thorndale Thorn*, June 2, 1911.

95   Williamson County, by the end of 1912, had spent $400,000 on macadam roads. Scarbrough, 351.

96   *Thorndale Thorn*, December 10, 1909; December 9, 1910.

97   *Thorndale Thorn*, April 15, 1910; September 9, 1910.

98   *Thorndale Thorn*, October 7, 1910; December 9, 1910; May 26, 1911.

99   *Thorndale Thorn*, February 3, 1911; March 17, 1911; March 24, 1911.

100   *Thorndale Thorn*, March 18, 1910; January 20, 1911; February 3, 1911.

101   *Thorndale Thorn*, May 27, 1904; June 29, 1906.

102   *Thorndale Thorn*, April 22, 1910; June 10 1910; June 16, 1911.

103   *Thorndale Thorn*, April 8, 1910; May 26, 1911.

104   *Thorndale Thorn*, December 14, 1907; October 28, 1910; May 5, 1911; June 9, 1910.

105   Arthur F. Raper, *The Tragedy of Lynching* (Chapel Hill: University of North Carolina Press, 1932), 6, 28.

106   *Texas Almanac*, 1911, 68.

107   *Thorndale Thorn*, July 29, 1904.

108   St. Paul congregation, on occasion, offered services in English on Wednesday nights. *Thorndale Thorn*, June 5, 1903.

CHAPTER IV. THORNDALE'S LEGACY OF VIOLENCE

109   Carl H. Moneyhon, *Texas after the Civil War: The Struggle of Reconstruction* (College Station: Texas A & M University Press, 2004), 29, 87–91.

110   Moneyhon, 115.

111   Lelia M. Batte, *History of Milam County, Texas* (San Antonio: The Naylor Company), 66, 67.

112   *Handbook of Texas Online, s.v.* "Davis, Edmund Jackson," http://www.tshaonline.org/handbook/online/articles/DD/fda37.html (accessed July 27, 2010); Robert M. Utley, *Lone Star Justice: The First Century of the Texas Rangers* (New York: Oxford University Press, 2002), 142; Moneyhon, 132, 139.

113   Allen G. Hatley, *Texas Constables: A Frontier Heritage* (Lubbock: Texas Tech University Press, 2006), 57.

114   Utley, 7, 34.

115   William C. Nunn, *Texas under the Carpetbaggers* (Austin: University of Texas Press, 1962), 191.

116   Utley, 137, 138.

117   Utley, 144, 145, 147.

118   Robert M. Utley, *Lone Star Lawmen: The Second Century of the Texas Rangers* (New York: Oxford University Press, 2007), 5.

119   Charles M. Robinson III, *The Men Who Wear the Star* (New York: Random House, 2000), 236, 239–240; *Handbook of Texas Online, s.v.* "Texas Rangers," http://www.tshaonline.org/handbook/online/articles/TT/met4.html (accessed July 27, 2010).

120   Utley, *Lone Star Lawmen,* 11; Hatley, 125, 126.

121   Walter P. Webb, *The Texas Rangers* (Austin: University of Texas Press, 1980); Julian Samora, Joe Bernal, and Albert Peña, *Gunpowder Justice: A Reassessment of the Texas Rangers* (Notre Dame, IN: University of Notre Dame Press, 1979); Utley, *Lone Star Justice,* 291–294.

122   Margaret Vandiver, *Lethal Punishment: Lynching and Legal Executions in the South* (New Brunswick, NJ: Rutgers University Press, 2006), 4; Christopher Waldrep, *The Many Faces of Judge Lynch: Extralegal Violence and Punishment in America* (New York: Palgrave Macmillan, 2002), 149; Philip Dray, *At the Hands of Persons Unknown: The Lynching of Black Americans* (New York: Random House, 2002), viii.

123   C. L. Sonnichsen, *I'll Die Before I'll Run* (New York: Harper & Brothers, 1951), xvi.; C. L. Sonnichsen, *10 Texas Feuds* (Albuquerque: University of New Mexico Press, 2000), 3, 5.

124   James R. McGovern, *Anatomy of a Lynching: The Killing of Claude Neal* (Baton Rouge: Louisiana State University Press, 1982), x.

125   Eliza Steelwater, *The Hangman's Knot: Lynching, Legal Executions, and America's Struggle with the Death Penalty* (Boulder, CO: Westview Press, 2003), 122, 130; Theodore Roosevelt, *Addresses and Presidential Messages of Theodore Roosevelt, 1902–1904* (New York, The Knickerbocker Press, 1904), 277.

126   Norton H. Moses, comp., in *Lynching and Vigilantism in the United States: An Annotated Bibliography* (Westport, CT: Greenwood Press, 1997), xiv, defines lynching as "a deliberate murder by a mob having a common purpose and targeting one or more previously specified individuals" and vigilantism as "the creation and enforcement of law by organized extra-legal groups in the supposed absence of adequate law enforcement."

127   Harry E. Chrisman, *The Ladder of Rivers: The Story of L. P. (Print) Olive* (Athens, OH: Swallow Press Books, 1962), 133, 180. Chrisman cites *Austin Statesman* of September 1, 1876.

128   Chrisman, 87–90.

129   Sonnichsen, 136, 137, 138; Chrisman, 144; *Handbook of Texas Online, s.v.* "Olive, Isom Prentice," http://www.tshaonline.org/handbook/online/articles/OO/fol12.html (accessed July 27, 2010).

130   Chrisman, 152, 182.

131   Chrisman, 132, 180, 383.

132   Published in San Francisco by History Company, 1887.

133   Richard Maxwell Brown, *Strains of Violence: Historical Studies of American Violence and Vigilantism* (New York: Oxford University Press, 1975), 96–97, 118, 126.

134   William D. Carrigan and Clive Webb, "The Lynching of Persons of Mexican Origin or Descent in the United States, 1848 to 1928," *Journal of Social History* (Winter 2003): 415.

135   Brown, 248–250.

136   *Bastrop Advertiser,* November 25, 1883 and *Galveston News* November 25, 1883; Wayne Schumpe, *et al.,* "Trinity Lutheran Church Fedor, Texas 1870–1995," (1995); George R. Nielsen, "Wendish Communities," *Texas Wendish Heritage Society Newsletter,* (January 2009): 4–5.

137   *Bastrop Advertiser,* December 1, 1883; January 26, 1884; *The Austin Daily Statesman,* December 26, 1883; December 27, 1883.

138   *The Austin Daily Statesman,* December 27, 1883.

139   Criminal Minutes Lee County District Court, July 16, 1874; December 14, 1874; May 5, 1886; Luise Maria Dressler, ed., *Mord in Texas: Erwin Wilhelm Mros Briefe,* (Frankfort-Main: n.p., 2008); *Texas Wendish Heritage Society Newsletter* (January 2009) 4–5.

140   *Rockdale Messenger,* April 27, 1899.

141   Brown, 103.

142   Brown, 21.

143   The *Chicago Tribune* began keeping records in 1882. Moses, xiv; *Handbook of Texas Online,* s.v. "Lynching," http://www.tshaonline.org/handbook/online/articles/LL/jgl1.html (accessed July 27, 2010).

144   Brown, 217–218; Amy Louise Wood, *Lynching and Spectacle: Witnessing Racial Violence in America, 1890–1940* (Chapel Hill: University of North Carolina Press, 2009), 1–7.

145   *Rockdale Reporter,* November 7, 1907.

146   *Rockdale Reporter and Messenger,* June 22, 1911. The owner in 1907 was R. W. H. Kennon and he sold the paper to John E. Cooke in June 1911.

147   William D. Carrigan, *The Making of a Lynching Culture* (Urbana: University of Illinois Press, 2004), 175.

CHAPTER V. THE ARRESTS AND TRIALS

148   William D. Carrigan and Clive Webb, "The Lynching of Persons of Mexican Origin or Descent in the United States, 1848 to 1928," *Journal of Social History* (Winter 2003): 417.

149   *San Antonio Express,* January 25, 1911.

150   Colquitt to W. W. Chambers, June 26, 1911, Records, Texas Governor Oscar B. Colquitt, Archives and Information Services Division, Texas State Library and Archives Commission. (Hereafter cited as ARIS-TESLAC).

151   H. P. N. Gammel, comp., *The Laws of Texas, 1822–1897* (Austin: The Gammel Book Co., 1898), 9: 829, 830.

152   Philip Dray, *At the Hands of Persons Unknown: The Lynching of Black Americans* (New York: Random House, 2002), ix.

153   C. E. Lane to Colquitt, July 1, 1911, Governor's Records, ARIS-TESLAC; Charles Harris and Louis Sadler, *The Texas Rangers and the Mexican Revolution: The Bloodiest Decade, 1910–1920* (Albuquerque: University of New Mexico Press, 2004), 73; *Cameron Daily Enterprise,* June 22, 1911, clipping, Acervo Histórico Diplomático, 4110-3, Archivo Histórico Genero Estrada, Secretaría de Relaciones Exteriores, Mexico City. (Hereafter cited as AHGE-SRE).

154   *The Daily Express* (San Antonio), July 25 and July 26, 1910; *San Antonio Express*, February 19, 1924; *Texas Almanac and State Industrial Guide for 1911* (Galveston: A. H. Belo & Company, 1911), 48; F. Arturo Rosales, *Chicano! The History of the Mexican American Civil Rights Movement* (Houston: Arte Público Press, 1996), 91.

155   F. A. Chapa to Colquitt, June 23, 1911; Colquitt to Col. F. A. Chappa [*sic*], June 23, 1911, Governor's Records, ARIS-TESLAC.

156   Colquitt to D. A. Divila [Davila], June 26, 1911, Governor's Records, ARIS-TESLAC; *San Antonio Light,* June 28, 1911.

157   *San Antonio Light*, June 25, 1911.

158   *The Rockdale Reporter and Messenger*, June 22, 1911.

159   *San Antonio Express*, June 25, 1911.

160   Acervo Histórico Diplomático, NC 110-3, AHGE-SRE

161   Ibid.

162   *Rockdale Reporter and Messenger,* June 29, 1911; *The Austin Daily Statesman*, June 25, 1911; *San Antonio Express,* June 25, 1911.

163   *New York Times*, June 26, 1911; *San Antonio Express,* June 24, 1911.

164   Eduardo Velardo Report, Acervo Histórico Diplomático, NC 110-3, AHGE-SRE; *New York Times*, June 26, 1911; *Austin Daily Statesman*, June 25, 1911; *San Antonio Express*, June 24, 1911.

165   Miguel E. Diebold to Colquitt, June 24, 1911; Colquitt to Miguel E. Diebold, June 26, 1911, Governor's Records, ARIS-TESLAC.

166   *Thorndale Thorn*, June 23, 1911.

167   Wilford Wilson to C. E. Lane, June 24, 1911; Colquitt to Wilford Wilson, June 27, 1911, Governor's Records, ARIS-TESLAC.

168   Colquitt to Allen Hooks, June 27, 1911; Allen Hooks to Colquitt, June 28, 1911, Governor's Records, ARIS-TESLAC.

169   *Cameron Daily Enterprise*, July 3, 1911.

170   *San Antonio Express*, August 2, 1911; Newspaper clipping August 3, 1911, in author's possession.

171   *Thorndale Thorn*, October 20, 1911; *Rockdale Reporter and Messenger*, October 26, 1911.

172   1910 U. S. Census, population schedule, Milam County, Texas, Precinct 8, Enumeration District 72, sheet 5, dwelling 97, family 98, Z. Taylor Gore household. Ancestry.com://www.ancestry.com (accessed January 26,2007); World War I Draft Registration Cards, 1917–1918, Milam County, Texas, Z. T. Gore, Jr., 1983490, Ancestry.com://www.ancestry.com (accessed January 26, 2007).

173   *San Antonio Express*, November 7, 1911.

174   *San Antonio Express*, November 9, 1911; *Rockdale Reporter and Messenger*, November 9, 1911; *San Antonio Express*, November 10, 1911.

175   *Thorndale Thorn*, April 8, 1910; June 5, 1903; November 3, 1911.

176   Harris and Sadler's identification of the pole as a light pole leaves the impression that identification of the members of the mob was not a problem. *The Texas Rangers*, 73.

177   Transcript, Acervo Histórico Diplomático, NC 110-3, AHGE-SRE; *San Antonio Express*, November 11, 1911.

178   *The State of Texas v. E. T. Gore, Jr.*, Milam County District Court, Criminal Minutes No. 7616, (November 13, 1911).

179   *San Antonio Express,* November 15, 1911; newspaper clipping November 16, 1911 in author's possession.

180   *The State of Texas v. Harry Wuensche,* Milam County District Court, Criminal Minutes No. 7614, (November 13, 1911).

181   *Thorndale Thorn,* December, 1, 1911. Newspaper clipping November 16, 1911; November 23, 1911, in author's possession.

182   Newspaper clipping February 1, 1912, in author's possession; *San Antonio Express,* November 18, 1911.

183   In 1904 he again ran for the position. 1880 U.S. Census, population schedule, Lee County, Texas, Precinct 2, Enumeration District 92, sheet 8 and 9, family 75, Christian Noack household. Ancestry.com://www.ancestry.com (accessed January 24, 2007); 1900 U. S. Census, population schedule, Fayette County, Texas, Precinct 4, Enumeration District 39, sheet 8, dwelling 149, family 149, Ernst Noack household. Ancestry.com://www.ancestry.com (accessed January 24, 2007); *Thorndale Thorn,* November 7, 1902; March 25, 1904.

184   *Thorndale Thorn,* April 8, 1910.

185   *Thorndale Thorn,* May 5, 1911. The family lived in a rented house.

186   *Williamson County Sun* (Georgetown), February 29, 1911.

187   Ibid.; Georgetown newspaper clipping May 2, 1912, in author's possession.

188   *The State of Texas v. G. P. Noack,* Williamson County District Court, Criminal Minutes No. 6767, (March 1, 1912).

189   Ibid.; *Williamson County Sun* (Georgetown), March 7, 1912.

190   *Thorndale Thorn,* September 9, 1910; September 23, 1910; October 7, 1910; October 21, 1910.

191   *Thorndale Thorn,* September 23, 1910; May 26, 1911; June 2, 1911; 1910 U. S. Census, population schedule, Milam County Texas, Precinct 8, Enumeration District 72, sheet 1, dwelling 5, family 5, William S. Stephens household. Ancestry.com://www.ancestry.com (accessed January 23, 2007).

192   Georgetown newspaper clipping May 2, 1912, in author's possession.

193   *Williamson County Sun* (Georgetown), May 16, 1912.

194   *San Antonio Express,* May 11, 1912; *Williamson County Sun* (Georgetown), May 16, 1912.

195   1910, U. S. Census, population schedule, Milam County, Texas, Precinct 8, Enumeration District 72, sheet 5, dwelling 103, family 104, Harry Wuensche household. Ancestry.com. (accessed January 23, 2007); *Thorndale Thorn,* February 25, 1910.

196   *Thorndale Thorn,* February 25, 1910; *Thorndale Thorn,* September 2, 1910.

197   *Thorndale Thorn,* December 23, 1910; July 21, 1911.

198   *Williamson County Sun* (Georgetown), June 6, 1912.

199   G. Biar to editor, *Giddings Deutsches Volksblatt,* July 6, 1911.

200   *San Antonio Express,* June 20, 1911.

201   *Williamson County Sun* (Georgetown), May 16, 1912.

202   *San Antonio Express,* June 20, 1911, quoted in *Rockdale Reporter and Messenger,* June 29, 1911; *Rockdale Reporter and Messenger,* June 22, 1911.

203   *Thorndale Thorn,* June 23, 1911; *San Antonio Express,* June 28, 1911.

CHAPTER VI. THE MEXICAN CONTEXT

204   Arnoldo De León, *They Called Them Greasers: Anglo Attitudes Toward Mexicans in Texas* (Austin: University of Texas Press, 1983), 104.

205   William D. Carrigan, *The Making of a Lynching Culture* (Urbana: University of Illinois Press, 2004), 177, 178.

206   1910 U. S. Census, population schedule, Milam County, Texas, Precinct 8, Enumeration District 72, sheet 6, dwelling 120, family 121, John Lyndecker household. Ancestry.com://www.ancestry.com (accessed January 15, 2007). Sixty-five blacks were farmers four were cooks, five laborers, and three were porters in hotels. Of the mulattos, ten were farmers and two were teachers.

207   1910 U. S. Census, population schedule, Milam County, Texas, Pct. 4, Enumeration District 62 and 64. Ancestry.com://www.ancestry.com (accessed January 18, 2007).

208   *Williamson County Sun* (Georgetown), February 29, 1912. "...One after another [of the jurors] was bowled out on the question of race."

209   David Montejano, *Anglos and Mexicans in the Making of Texas, 1836–1986* (Austin: University of Texas Press, 1987), 143; *Handbook of Texas Online*, s.v. "White Man's Union Associations," http://www.tshaonline.org/handbook/online/articles/WW/vcw2.html (accessed July 28, 2010); "White Primary," http://www.tshaonline.org/handbook/online/articles/WW/wdw1.html (accessed July 28, 2010); *Thorndale Thorn*, July 17, 1904. Discrimination by color was not a phenomenon limited to the United States. In September 1910 Porfiro Díaz arranged for the celebration of Mexico's one hundredth anniversary of independence and his own eightieth birthday, and to impress foreign dignitaries Díaz ordered the employers of hotels and restaurants that catered to foreign visitors to employ light skinned Mexicans. Idar resented Mexicans being tied to blacks. *La Crónica (Laredo)*, June 29, 1911.

210   Richard Gambino, *Vendetta: A True Story of the Worst Lynching in America* (Garden City, NY: Doubleday & Company, 1977), 82–87, 93–95, 117–128.

211   Anita Brenner and George R. Leighton, *The Wind that Swept Mexico: The History of the Mexican Revolution of 1910–1942* (Austin: University of Texas Press, 1971); Stanley R. Ross, *Franciso I. Madero: Apostle of Mexican Democracy* (New York: Columbia University Press, 1955); Michael C. Meyer and William H. Beezley, eds., *The Oxford History of Mexico* (New York: Oxford University Press, 2000), 435–466.

212   *New York Times*, November 11, 1910; Charles Harris and Louis Sadler, *The Texas Rangers and the Mexican Revolution: The Bloodiest Decade, 1910–1920* (Albuquerque: University of New Mexico Press, 2004), 51.

213   Harvey F. Rice, "The Lynching of Antonio Rodríguez," (M.A. thesis, University of Texas, 1990), 24, 90–94.

214   June 22, 1911.

215   William D. Carrigan and Clive Webb, "The Lynching of Persons of Mexican Origin or Descent in the United States," *Journal of Social History* (Winter 2003): 428; José E. Limón, "El Primer Congreso Mexicanista de 1911: A Precursor to Contemporary Chicanismo," Aztlán (1974): 88; F. Arturo Rosales, *¡Pobre Raza! Violence, Justice, and Mobilization among Mexico Lindo Immigrants, 1900–1936* (Austin: University of Texas Press, 1999), 37.

216   *La Crónica* (Laredo), June 29, 1911.

217   *La Crónica* (Laredo), June 29, 1911; July 13, 1911.

218   Eduardo Velardo Report, Acervo Histórico Diplomático, NC 4110-3, Archivo Histórico Genero Estrada, Secretaría de Relaciones Exteriores, Mexico City. (Hereafter cited as AHGE-SRE).

219   Peter V. H. Henderson, *In the Absence of Don Porfirio: Francisco León de la Barra and the Mexican Revolution* (Wilmington, DE: S. R. Books, 2000), 30, 31, 138.

220   Harris, 52; Julian Samora, et al., *Gunpowder Justice: A Reassessment of the Texas Rangers* (Notre Dame, IN: University of Notre Dame Press, 1979), 63. The Rodríguez family in Coahuila received some indemnification from the Mexican government. Rosales, *¡Pobre Raza!*, 37.

221   Francisco H. Vázquez and Rodolfo D. Torres, *Latino/a Thought: Culture, Politics, and Society* (Lanham, MD: Rowman & Littlefield, 2002), 222, 223; *Handbook of Texas Online*, s.v. "Idar, Nicasio," http://www.tshaonline.org/handbook/online/articles/II/fid2.html (accessed July 28, 2010); Limón, 87.

222   *Handbook of Texas Online*, s.v. "Mexican-American Land Grant Adjudication," http://www.tshaonline.org/handbook/online/articles/MM/pqmck.html (accessed July 28, 2010).

223   Montejano, 114, 115; *Handbook of Texas Online,* "Mexican-American Land Grant Adjudication."

224   Robert Utley, *Lone Star Lawmen: The Second Century of the Texas Rangers* (New York: Oxford University Press, 2007), 13–15; Montejano, 50.

225   Limón 87–88; *La Crónica* (Laredo), June 29, 1911; Montejano, 92, 115.

226   Utley, 13. The Mexican consul at Del Rio complained to the United States State Department that he had been attacked by some Madero supporters. The Secretary of State forwarded the letter to Governor Colquitt who in turn referred the issue to the sheriff of Val Verde County. Colquitt commented: "I have found that upon investigation, as you doubtless observed, many of the complaints by the Mexican officials result from frivolous matters." Colquitt to P. C. Knox, June 23, 1911, Records, Texas Governor Oscar B. Colquitt, Archives and Information Services Division, Texas State Library and Archives Commission. (Hereafter cited as ARIS-TESLAC.)

227   De León, 104.

228   Harris, 17. The word *"rinches"* was derived from "Rangers" but evolved into a derogatory term. Samora, 41.

229   *Texas Almanac and State Industrial Guide for 1911* (Galveston: A. H. Belo & Company, 1911), 30; Utley, 3, 8, 10, 11.

230   Utley, 5.

231   Montejano, 116.

232   Limón, 91, 92; *Handbook of Texas Online, s.v.* "Congreso Mexicanista," tshaonline.org/handbook/online/articles/CC/vecyk.html (accessed February 8, 2008); David J. Weber, ed., *Foreigners in Their Native Land: Historical Roots of the Mexican Americans* (Albuquerque: University of New Mexico Press, 1973), 249. The slogan was similar to "All for one and one for all."

233   *La Crónica* (Laredo), July 13, 1911.

234   *La Crónica* (Laredo), June 29, 1911.

235   Montejano, 116, 117; Weber, 248–9.

236   Carrigan and Webb, 426.

237   Carrigan and Webb, 427.

238   *La Crónica* (Laredo), June 29, 1911.

239   Diebold as a trusted "right hand man" of Díaz was sent to San Antonio because it was the headquarters of the revolutionaries. *San Antonio Light,* May 3, 1911; May 7, 1911.

240   Diebold Report, June 28, 1911, Acervo Histórico Diplomático, NC 4110-3, AHGE-SRE.

241   *San Antonio Light,* June 28, 1911.

242   *San Antonio Light,* June 26, 1911; June 27, 1911; Colquitt to D. A. Divila [Davila], June 26, 1911, Governor's Records, ARIS-TESLAC.

243   *San Antonio Light,* June 28, 1911; Broadside, Acervo Histórico Diplomático, NC 4110 -3, AHGE-SRE.

244   *San Antonio Light,* July 2, 1911.

245   Lane to M. A. Esteva, August 15, 1911, Acervo Histórico Diplomático, NC 4110 -3, AHGE-SRE.

246   *La Crónica* (Laredo), June 29, 1911.

247   *La Crónica* (Laredo), June 29, 1911.

248   *San Antonio Light,* June 22, 1911.

249   *La Crónica* (Laredo), June 29. 1911; F. Arturo Rosales, *Chicano! The History of the Mexican American Civil Rights Movement* (Houston: Arte Público Press, 1996), 60–61.

250   Holt Reinhart and Winston, "Formal Response to Written Testimony" [about a text book, *American Government*] August 23, 2002. Holt's response was that they covered the Mexican civil rights issue in their history text. ritter. tea.state.tx.us/textbooks/adopt process/aug_holt2.pdf, (accessed January 15, 2010).

251   Carrigan, 175; F. Arturo Rosales, *Dictionary of Latino Civil Rights History* (Houston: Arte Público Press, 2006), 184; Arnoldo de León, *Mexican Americans in Texas: A Brief History,* 2nd ed. (Wheeling, IL: Harlan Davidson, 1999), 50, 51; Limón, 88.

CHAPTER VII. AFTERMATH

252   William D. Carrigan and Clive Webb, "The Lynching of Persons of Mexican Origins or Descent in the United States, 1848–1928," *Journal of Social History* (Winter 2003): 411; Mamie Till-Mobley, *The Death of Innocence: The Story of the Hate Crime that Changed America* (New York: Random House, 2003).

253   David C. Chapman, "Lynching in Texas," (Master's Thesis, Texas Tech University, August 1973), 78, 82 etd.lib.ttu.edu/thesis/available/etd (accessed January 22, 2009).

254   Richard Maxwell Brown, *Strain of Violence: Historical Studies of American Violence and Vigilantism* (New York: Oxford University Press, 1975), 151, 217; Handbook of Texas Online, s.v. "Lynching," http://www.tshaonline.org/handbook/online/articles/LL/jgl1.html (accessed August 5, 2010).

255   Eliza Steelwater, *The Hangman's Knot: Lynching, Legal Executions, and America's Struggle with the Death Penalty* (Boulder: Westview Press, 2003);

Michael J. Pfeifer, *Rough Justice: Lynching and American Society, 1874–1947* (Urbana: University of Illinois Press, 2004), 152–153.

256   *Rockdale Reporter and Messenger,* June 22, 1911; The *San Antonio Express* wrote "Mobocracy is anarchy." June 24, 1911.

257   *Thorndale Thorn,* June 20, 1911; June 23, 1911; *Taylor Journal,* June 22, 1911.

258   *Rockdale Reporter and Messenger,* June 29, 1911.

259   Chapman, 82; G. E. Grider was employed by the Mexican government not take part in the trial, but to ensure compliance with all laws and that the case would be actively prosecuted. *Williamson County Sun,* March 7, 1912. While most of the lynching examples were associated with lynching of blacks, Carrigan and Webb, who examined lynching of Mexicans, largely credit diplomatic efforts. "More than any other form of resistance, it was ultimately the diplomatic protests of the Mexican government that proved decisive in the decline of violence." 411, 427.

260   *Giddings Deutsches Volksblatt,* July 6, 1911.

261   Gamez Statement, Acervo Histórico Diplomático, NC4110-3. Archivo Histórico Genero Estrada, Secretaría de Relaciones Exteriores, Mexico City. (Hereafter cited as AHGE-SRE). Gamez includes details of the lynching given by him to Antonio Alvarez, supposedly an eye-witness. The numerous inaccuracies make his presence at the lynching doubtful and he was never mentioned in the testimony.

262   *San Antonio Light,* June 27, 1911.

263   Acervo Histórico Diplomático, 4110-4, General Claims Arbitration, Docket No. 914, AHGE-SRE.

264   1920 U. S. Census, population schedule, Wichita County, Texas, Precinct 1, Enumeration District 119, sheet 30, dwelling 415, family 552, Samuel Gilpin household. Ancestry.com://www.ancestry.com (accessed November 14, 2009).

265   World War I Draft Registration Cards 1917–1918, Jefferson County, Texas, roll number 1953882, Ancestry.com://www.ancestry.com (accessed November 14, 2009); 1920 U. S. Census, population schedule, Liberty County, Texas, Precinct 5, Enumeration District 129, sheet 1, dwelling 2, family 2, G. P. Noack household. Ancestry.com://www.ancestry.com (accessed November 5, 2009).

266   World War I Draft Registration Cards 1917–1918, Milam County, Texas, roll number 1983490, Ancestry.com://www.ancestry.com (accessed November 10, 2009; 1920 U. S. Census, population schedule, Thorndale, Milam County, Texas, Enumeration District 137, sheet 1, dwelling 22, family 22, Mattie Stevens [sic] household. Ancestry.com://www.ancestry.com (accessed November 7, 2009); 1930 U. S, Census, population schedule, Corpus Christi, Texas, Nueces County, Texas, Enumeration District 178-3, sheet 6, dwelling 99, household 139, Ezra Stephens household, Ancestry.com://www.ancestry.com (accessed November 24, 2009); Family tree maker.com

267   *Thorndale Thorn*, November 19, 1909; February 3, 1911.

268   Abilene State School History, dad.state,tx.us/services/state schools/Abilene/about.html (accessed October 10, 2005); 1920 U. S. Census, population schedule, Taylor County, Texas, precinct 1, Enumeration District 258, sheet 5, dwelling 28, family 28, Charley Linn household. Ancestry.com://www.ancestry.com (accessed November 14, 2009).

269   *Handbook of Texas Online*, s.v. "Chapa, Francisco A.," http://www.tshaonline.org/handbook/online/articles/CC/fch50.html (accessed July 28, 2010); Charles H. Harris III and Lewis R. Sadler, "The 1911 Reyes Conspiracy: The Texas Side," *The Southwestern Historical Quarterly* (April 1988), 332.

270   *With His Pistol in His Hand: A Border Ballad and Its Hero* (Austin: University of Texas Press, 1958), 97.

271   Colquitt to Col. F. A. Chappa [*sic*] June 23, 1911, Records, Texas Governor Oscar B. Colquitt, Archives and Information Services Division, Texas State Library and Archives Commission; *San Antonio Express*, December 12, 1911; February 19, 1924; F. Arturo Rosales, *Chicano!: The History of the Mexican American Civil Rights Movement* (Houston: Arte Público Press, 1996), 91, 92.

272   *San Antonio Express*, July 23, 1911; *San Antonio Light*, October 6, 1911.

273   World War I Draft Registration Cards, 1917–1918, Harris County, Texas, registration number 1953562. Ancestry.com://www.ancestry.com (accessed November 12, 2009); 1930 U. S. Census, population schedule, Williamson County, Texas, Enumeration District 20, sheet 2, dwelling 46, family 54, Wilford Wilson household. Ancestry.com://www.ancestry.com (accessed November 7, 2007).

274   John S. Spratt, *The Road to Spindletop: Economic Change in Texas 1875–1901* (Dallas: Southern Methodist University Press, 1955), 283. Diana Davids Olien and Roger M. Olien, *Oil in Texas, the Gusher Age 1895–1945* (Austin: University of Texas Press, 2002), 116.

275   1920 U. S. Census, population schedule, Thorndale, Milam County, Texas, Enumeration District 137, sheets 1–25. Ancestry.com://www.ancestry. com (accessed November 20, 2009)

276   When national prohibition ended, the sale of alcohol once more became a local issue. As a school child in the early 1940s I stopped by at a gasoline station near our home. The owner was reading the newspaper announcing another local option election. He was confused about voting and said, "Run home and ask your daddy that if I want beer, should I vote for or against prohibition."

277   Sanford maps are available at most large municipal libraries.

Index

O

Olive, Bob 71
Olive family 36, 70, 71
Olive, Isom Prentice 24, 37, 71
Olive, James 24, 72
Olive, Jay 71

P

Penny, G. W. 5, 6, 8, 10, 85, 87, 88, 89, 91, 98
Perkinson, G. L. 86, 90
Pichardo, José Antonio 17
Poldrack, Ernest 71
Polnick, A. E. 73
Polnick, C. A. 37
Prohibition 81, 127

Q

Quinn, James K. 42

R

racial discrimination xii, 90, 96, 100, 101, 102
railroads
  convict labor 26
  economic impact 31
  funding 25, 29
  post Civil War Texas 26
Ramsey, E. L. 46, 51, 120
Rangers
  as police officers 66
  early history 65
  historical interpretations 68
  Mexican border 110
  Mexican Revolution 107
road improvement 53
Rockdale, Texas xiii, 3, 6, 27, 28, 30, 31, 32, 38, 39, 40, 45, 51, 57, 77, 101, 120, 133, 139, 140, 141, 143, 148
Rock Springs, Texas 104, 105, 112
Rodríguez, Antonio 104, 105, 106, 111, 118, 144, 145

S

San Antonio, Texas 9, 11, 19, 21, 82, 83, 84, 90, 97, 106, 107, 109, 113, 116, 121, 123, 124, 125, 129, 134, 137, 139, 140, 141, 142, 143, 146, 147, 148, 149
Sanborn Fire Insurance Map Company 127
Scott, J. C. 77, 85, 89
Serbin, Texas 35, 36, 37, 38, 94, 133
Soder, Fedor 37, 73
Stephens, Ezra 7, 8, 55, 57, 84, 88, 89, 91, 92, 93, 94, 124, 142, 149
  trial of 91
Stephens, William S. 2, 91, 101

T

Taylor, Texas 3, 6, 10, 31, 36, 38, 53, 55, 57, 59, 87, 90, 123, 130, 134, 141, 148, 149
Texas Land Company 29, 131
Texas State Rangers 67, 110
Thorndale
  beautification 59
  brick construction 47
  cotton gins 49
  early growth 43
  electricity 58
  founding 42
  merchandise 43
  newspaper 46
  oil mill 50, 51
  Opera House 49
  petroleum 126
  sidewalks 59
  social divisions 60
  telephone 57
  water supply 42, 45, 46
Thrall, Texas 31, 36, 54, 126
Tuskegee Institute 76, 119

V

Velardo, Eduardo 84, 101, 113, 123
vigilantism 74
  historical interpretations 72
  protocol 75
violence
  Reconstruction 63, 64

W

Watson, J. L. 7, 8, 9, 83
Wends 33, 34, 35, 36, 37, 38, 61, 71,
      73, 94, 109, 117, 132, 133
Wilcox, C. A. 90
Williamson County 16
  cattle trade 22, 24, 70
  cotton 32
  formation 19
  Mexican presence 38
  population 32
  soils and vegetation 22
  violence 67, 70
Wilson, Wilford 4, 5, 6, 7, 8, 9, 10, 58,
      84, 85, 86, 87, 91, 98, 126, 132,
      133, 141, 149
Wuensche, Charles 94
Wuensche, Harry 7, 8, 38, 57, 84, 88,
      94, 95, 124, 125, 142, 143
  case dismissed 95

Z

Zieschang, Carl 35, 37
Zieschang, Charles (Karl) 1, 2, 3, 4, 5,
      8, 9, 10, 11, 12, 15, 35, 37, 38,
      44, 54, 55, 57, 58, 71, 78, 79,
      83, 86, 89, 96, 117, 121, 133
  death of 3
Zieschang, Johann 35, 37
Zieschang, John 15
Zieschang, Peter 35, 36, 37, 71